THE UNIQUE INDIVIDUAL

BY

JOHNSON O'CONNOR

HUMAN ENGINEERING LABORATORY
INCORPORATED

THE UNIQUE INDIVIDUAL
First Edition 1948
50,000 copies

This brochure replaces
CHARACTERISTICS COMMON TO PROFESSIONAL MEN
IN NON-STRUCTURAL FIELDS

JOHNSON O'CONNOR RESEARCH FOUNDATION INCORPORATED
11 East Sixty Second Street New York 21 New York
(*Formerly at Stevens Institute of Technology Hoboken New Jersey*)

HUMAN ENGINEERING LABORATORY INCORPORATED
347 Beacon Street Boston 16 Massachusetts
(*Formerly at 381 Beacon Street*)
172 Chestnut Street Springfield Massachusetts

HUMAN ENGINEERING LABORATORY
2012 Delancey Place Philadelphia 3 Pennsylvania
(*Formerly at Chestnut Hill Academy*)

675 Rush Street Chicago 11 Illinois
(*Formerly at Illinois Institute of Technology
Glessner House 1800 Prairie Avenue*)

1880 Arcade Building Saint Louis 1 Missouri
(*Formerly at 3607 Olive Street*)

1403 Riverside Drive Tulsa 3 Oklahoma
(*Formerly at 703 Boston Building*)

218 Majestic Building Fort Worth 2 Texas
(*Formerly at 1409 Sinclair Building*)

1388 Filbert Street San Francisco 9 California

Park View Building 2404 West Seventh Street Los Angeles 5 California

CONTENTS

TABLES

FIGURES

STAFF

Johnson O'Connor, DIRECTOR

Boston

Bette Bailey
Alice A. Bartlett
Anson M. Dubois
John F. Given

Talbot Fancher Hamlin
Paula G. Knight
Margaret A. Langille
Gail Peterson

Chicago

Jane A. Bittel
Patricia M. Pryor
Ruth Schulte

Fort Worth

Eleanor Bowers
Caroline Dowlen
Dean Trembly

Los Angeles

Elizabeth F. Edwards
Virginia A. Holman

Mary E. Richards
Billie F. Woodard

New York

Elizabeth Bixby
Edith Callaghan
Tina Carbonaro
Carol Agnes Crissey
Joanne Greene

Wilfrid Hamlin
Betty Jane Killenberger
Helen Merritt
Lillian Quesnel

Corinne Solow
Valerie Stevens
Virginia Turner
Sylvia Ward
Esther Woodburn

Philadelphia

Achsah Darnell
Nancy Fitts
Kathryn Harriman

Marie H. Licht
Eleanora C. Marston
Ruth Reshall

San Francisco
Winifred Sorensen

Springfield
Amy Corkum

St. Louis
Esther H. Moore

Tulsa

Barbara Dille

Kathryn Fell

SUBJECTIVE PERSONALITY

Three-quarters of all men and women belong by nature to one personality type, the remainder to another. From the objective multitude come prosperous business men, from the extremely subjective minority come creative artists, gifted writers, lyric poets, scrupulous surgeons, diligent scientists, and unworldly musicians. The easy momentum of the conservative majority carries the civilized world from day to day, as a revolving fly wheel, once in heavy motion, carries a reciprocating engine smoothly past each successive stalling point; while the explosive minority furnish the impulsive driving force.

In the considered choice of a lifelong career, men and women who score extremely subjective must face the disadvantages of belonging to the outnumbered species. In place of counting on the established three-quarters duplicating their own emotional reactions, they gain their point only by anticipatory study and such prudent presentation that every verdict rests on a rational consideration of the controversial issue. For this reason, extremely subjective persons thrive in fields of trained advice, as in the practice of medicine, legal counseling, engineering design, certified public accounting, and the fine arts, and only occasionally enjoy the jostling business world.

Extreme subjectivity strives obstinately toward an enduring goal, a better mankind, where lasting progress is not easy, innovations remorselessly criticized, professional standards not raised without a disheartening struggle. An extremely subjective embittered dentist, who sought consolation from many quarters, begged to unburden his rankling anxieties. It bothered him to gain so little pleasure from normal living. High in structural visualization, he developed a mechanical technique which he felt would mitigate adult troubles if applied to growing children. But professional opposition, buttressed by public indifference toward his all-absorbing interest, drove him to a despondent state of nervous exhaustion. Temperamentally

irritated by his own inability to impress upon complacent
parents the need of obviating in childhood the troubles he met
later, he finally despaired and longed to live contentedly like
others of his suburban community. Knowing that he could
never accept such lay advice, the administrator suggested that
he forego pioneering and practice his calling, where in the
public mind he was unquestionably successful. But he insisted
that he could belong to no group without raising its standards;
nor could he see innocent children suffer without struggling
to remedy the incipient evil

After reading the disconcerting biography of Wolfgang
Mozart, this middle-west dentist felt little sympathy for the
Austrian composer's blind allegiance to aesthetic creation; and
yet he saw the same symptoms in himself, knew that great
scientists, glorious artists, and sublime musicians live turbulent
lives, but leave behind illustrious works which raise human
happiness to a new level. He typifies the extremely subjective
person who sacrifices himself irresistibly to a visionary principle, who suffers in so doing, whose inner nature pushes him
remorselessly to the precipitous verge of a mental breakdown,
but who cannot desist; for the extremely subjective person
contributes lastingly to human welfare at the expense of his
own immediate comfort. To win the profound gratification
which this man craved, he would not for a moment forsake
his fantastic ambition. Fundamentally he demands speedier
progress, an achievement which depends upon still greater
sacrifice. The Laboratory can disclose the concrete facts,
lighten a bit the chimerical burden by showing the total
situation; but it cannot simplify human attainment, and nothing
less compensates extreme subjectivity.

One must guard against some phantom aim drawing toward
an urgent reform for which one has no gift; for the rudimentary steps toward a happier race have all been taken, and only
tangible accomplishments, gained through picturing a problem
and preparing for its solution with impersonal detachment,
satisfy the missionary spirit. Turning to cooperative buying
because he failed the introductory nonstructural rote portions
of organic chemistry, a premedical student, high in structural
visualization, deserted his goal, and nothing short of four years'

fruitless effort convinced him that he lacked every business requisite. Tested for the first time at this point, he scored like the surgeon, table ɪ. Cooperative buying requires objectivity, and he scored extremely subjective, demands high creative imagination, and he scored low. He saw in cooperative buying

TABLE I

SURGERY VERSUS COOPERATIVE BUYING

MEASURED TRAITS	COOPERATIVE BUYING	SURGERY	THIS BOY'S INVENTORY
personality	objective	extremely subjective	extremely subjective
creative imagination	high	low	low
structural visualization	low	high	high
tweezer dexterity	low	high	high

EVERY PERSON TESTED SHOULD LIST HIS OWN RESULTS COMPARED WITH THE PRESUMED PATTERN FOR EACH OCCUPATION AND PROFESSION HE IS CONSIDERING. CONSULT THE INDEX UNDER OCCUPATIONS AND UNDER EACH APTITUDE.

the same chance to help humanity which first attracted him to medicine, where he should have continued despite the minor inevitable setbacks which everyone encounters.

To meet the ubiquitous problem of earning a living and supporting a family, the extremely subjective man may turn temporarily to business for its financial returns; but for continued happiness he must not be drawn into the hectic struggle for money and executive position, but regard himself as an independent individualist, unswervingly loyal to art which never forgives time wasted in mercantile climbing.

A slender, quiet, aesthetic, high-school freshman asked if his potential ability warranted his persevering at commercial advertising. His ingratiating personality and supple stature will bring advancements in both salary and organization responsibilities until, by casual degrees, he regards himself as a budding executive, rather than a striving artist; and then, too late for retreat, he senses the unhappy dichotomy which terminates in mediocrity, for this boy scores as shown in table II. Commercial design, countenanced too readily by parents who believe that it gives aesthetic satisfaction together with financial security, demands an objective personality. The extremely sub-

TABLE II

APTITUDES WHICH SUGGEST MUSICAL PERFORMANCE

extremely subjective	in personality
high (99th percentile)	in tweezer dexterity
high (80th percentile)	in finger dexterity
average (60th percentile)	in tonal memory
average (55th percentile)	in abstract visualization
average (50th percentile)	in accounting aptitude
average (46th percentile)	in structural visualization
low (10th percentile)	in ideaphoria
low (5th percentile)	in English vocabulary

THIS HIGH-SCHOOL FRESHMAN BELONGS SOMEWHERE IN MUSICAL PERFORMANCE; NOT IN COMMERCIAL DESIGN, WHICH DEMANDS OBJECTIVITY AND IDEAPHORIA.

jective child detests a compromise and gains greater ultimate satisfaction by concentrating an undivided mind and physique on scaling the precipitous heights of pure art.

With this same high-school freshman low creative imagination, now called ideaphoria, pulls against commercial art, table III, toward performance rather than design. Based solely on aptitudes the concert piano seems likely to embrace his total pattern; for just below his two dexterities, vital factors in the graphic arts, his tonal memory suggests music. The father, a music connoisseur, describes the boy's touch as exquisite. While success checks with using aptitudes in their relative order, this serious-minded boy scores only at the 60th percentile in tonal memory. Is this high enough to justify a field risky to stress with anyone not already inspired? The boy's drawback is of course his low English vocabulary, below the 5th percentile, so low that he cannot comprehend the rare prospects of his endowments, a synthesis of music and art, perhaps in motion-pictures or somewhere in the theater.

Coming to see if his interest in the fine arts had substantial foundation, a bespectacled high-school sophomore showed the aptitude pattern of the professional photographer, table IV. Bits of evidence suggest that pitch discrimination and perchance tonal memory, while called musical traits, may be

TABLE III

PROBABLE TRAITS OF THE COMMERCIAL ARTIST
WHO RISES TO ADVERTISING EXECUTIVE

objective	personality
high	ideaphoria
high	abstract visualization
high	memory for design
high	proportion appraisal
low	structural visualization
very high	English vocabulary
high	vocabulary of art
high	knowledge of paintings

THE SUBJECTIVE BOY SHOULD REGARD HIMSELF AS AN ARTIST, NOT AS A POTENTIAL EXECUTIVE, THOUGH HE EARN A LIVING AT COMMERCIAL ART.

aspects of some general niceness of sense perception, for both amateur and commercial photographers score high. Finger dexterity the boy would use in either creative art or in photography. Observation he would unquestionably use in both. In personality, worksample 35 form AE, he scored near enough the crucial division between seven and eight significant responses so that the difference may be a test inaccuracy, for artists score extremely subjective. The danger is that a boy with these aptitudes acquires art techniques easily and may then have nothing to express. For encouragement he should continue art, experiment with photography. To alleviate his low accounting aptitude, likely to push him away from languages, he belongs in a small school, with a total of less than seventy pupils. To build continuously from his 5th percentile vocabulary level, he belongs in one recently founded. To support himself financially in any field, including art, he must pursue his study of words, their meanings, and literary use.

As a boy regards some eccentric course, the inevitable conflict of the pioneering appetite and the well-intentioned scruples of a reactionary world warp his own instinctive judgment. The top four aptitudes of a high-school senior, table v, indicate music. He wants radio announcing, an ideal outlet; but a

TABLE IV

ApproxiMATE TRAITS OF THE PROFESSIONAL PHOTOGRAPHER

high (80th percentile)	pitch discrimination
high (75th percentile)	finger dexterity
high (72nd percentile)	observation
average (65th percentile)	tonal memory
very low (below 5th percentile)	accounting aptitude
probably objective	personality
(10 significant responses, form AE)	

PITCH DISCRIMINATION, AND TO A LESSER EXTENT THE MUSICAL TRAIT, TONAL MEMORY, CHARACTERIZE BOTH AMATEUR AND PROFESSIONAL PHOTOGRAPHERS, AND HIGH PRECISION LENSE GRINDERS, AS WELL AS MUSICIANS.

worried father naturally wonders at mention of so precarious a calling. Parental prejudice against the arts where this kind of boy has his greatest opportunity rests upon the very feature which makes them suitable, their unusualness; for the extremely subjective minority, especially for those low in accounting aptitude and low in structural visualization, the little known job offers overwhelmingly the best statistical chances. Such a boy comes to learn his measured aptitudes and need follow the findings only if he so chooses. In this instance the parents originally wanted their son in banking or accounting but, in response to a national call for engineers, shifted their emphasis to technical aeronautics.

To the worldly eye public accounting and airplane design are mapped highways where a normal boy with basic training earns a steady living. Both satisfy this boy's extreme subjectivity, and the Laboratory hesitates to reject either. But judged by aptitudes his prospects are slim in either business or engineering. Only three per cent of examinees low in accounting aptitude survive in accounting eight years or longer, compared with eighty per cent of those who score high. Were this boy's father an established accountant, or were the boy uniformly low in many aptitudes so that he had no better chance elsewhere, he might reasonably try the profession, against heavy actuarial odds. In designing engineering, where the boy could use both

TABLE V

Aptitudes sanction Radio Announcing

IN FAVOR OF MUSIC:

high	in tonal memory
high	in pitch discrimination
high	in creative imagination
extremely subjective	in personality

AGAINST ENGINEERING:

low	in structural visualization

AGAINST BANKING:

low	in accounting aptitude

THE DESIRE OF THIS HIGH-SCHOOL SENIOR TO TRY RADIO ANNOUNCING SEEMED FANTASTIC TO HIS PARENTS, WHO HAD SET THEIR HEARTS ON BANKING OR ENGINEERING; BUT APTITUDE SCORES CONFIRM HIS JUDGMENT OF HIMSELF.

ideaphoria and extreme subjectivity, only two in a hundred low in structural visualization last five years compared with seventy in a hundred high in the same trait. Yet any composite description, based upon averaging numbers, departs in detail from each actual case. With its years of experience and accumulated statistics, the Laboratory advises a hundred persons with justified confidence, but the individual examinee who receives this brochure at the conclusion of his appointment must not expect each phrase to fit himself perfectly.

Counting on physical comfort and freedom from money worries to reward them for time spent in distasteful surroundings, extremely subjective persons who assay commerce for its seemingly rich rewards seldom reach the anticipated contentment. After a year and a half as district manager of a western organization which bought the drawing power of his name, gained on the baseball diamond, an extremely subjective man, familiar to every sports enthusiast, resigned despite abundant financial recompense, and returned to college for a law degree. Subsequently admitted to the bar, an overpowering money offer coerced him back to business, which eight years later failed to give what he had hoped from life, and he came to be tested. His lithe body and heavy frame lent

TABLE VI

APTITUDE PATTERN OF A PROFESSIONAL ACCOUNTANT

extremely subjective	personality
(3 significant responses on form AE)	
high	accounting aptitude
high	abstract visualization
average or high	analytical reasoning
low	ideaphoria
low	structural visualization

THESE ARE THE APTITUDE SCORES OF AN ACCOUNTANT WHO ACCEPTED WHAT SEEMED TO HIM ADVANCEMENT TO PERSONNEL MANAGER AND WHO, AFTER AN UNHAPPY TEN YEARS, LOST HIS POSITION DURING A GENERAL DEPRESSION.

him the outward mein of easy objectivity; his dissatisfaction hinged on his extremely subjective score in worksample 35, a single significant response to form FK, and none to form AE. On the baseball diamond he throve on the adulation of the crowd. Then the legal profession drew his subjective personality from a comfortable industrial salary to college; and later still unsatisfied he came from his executive desk to the Laboratory. Lavish earnings never reimbursed this man for the sacrifice of his personality to business.

Recognizing a natural vexation at any reflection on his commercial acumen, the extremely subjective man, in business through force of circumstances, should face honestly his own personality type or may find it drawing him toward progressively less comfortable situations. Sought out by fellow members of his own department, a tall, thin accountant of thirty-five made an unofficial reputation for straightening out personnel problems and in reward was appointed personnel manager of a wire mill's four thousand employees. While the Laboratory has no scientifically validated pattern, for the approach to personnel varies with each person, the work seems to use objectivity and ideaphoria, where this man scores extremely subjective and low, as he should for accounting. Ten years later, admitting that employment records were never in better shape, the management complained that the man contributed nothing to the negotiation of labor contracts, was not diplomatic with aggrieved employees, and lavished time on clerical details, seldom leaving his own private office. When tested at forty-five he scored as shown in table VI, an aptitude set which explained in retrospect what had happened. His high accounting aptitude established him firmly in the accounting department. His extreme subjectivity lent an interest in individuals and he dealt sympathetically with subjective colleagues. He should have mounted to chief accountant of the local plant, thence to the general accounting department of the national organization, and finally to comptroller, treasurer, or financial vice-president, continuing to sympathize with fellow workers but holding accounting as his major aim. Instead he allowed his feeling for human problems to lead him to the personnel managership, which he lost after ten years, at the age of forty-five, during a general depression when he found it impossible to make another connection.

As the two-tined title: COMMERCIAL DESIGN decoys the visionary artist into the brittle bustle of an advertising office, and the word PERSONNEL leads the bland humanitarian mistakenly into business, so the reverse may happen and the term SELLING divert the extremely subjective person from a happy choice. When a subordinate, solely responsible for the sale of a million dollars of fabrics annually, scored extremely subjective, a brusque sales employer questioned the personality worksample with the glib statement that a few such men, each selling a like amount, would distribute his gross output. To hiring extremely subjective salesmen for the purpose he uttered the obvious answer that no similar opening existed. The million-dollar man made no new business contacts, brought in no fresh customers, but sold to a single large retail distributor, owned primarily by the controlling shareholders of his own organization. His duty was to offer friendly service, devoting his life to the furtherance of pleasant relationships between associates.

In many industrial set-ups so-called line positions take objectivity. In a large oil company, nine district sales managers report to a general sales manager who, in turn **STAFF AND LINE** with others of his own rank, two handling **ORGANIZATIONS** foreign sales and one in charge of government contracts, work for the sales vice-president. Lower in the line, beneath every district sales manager, come a dozen or more sales managers, and under these in turn local managers. Each plays an integral part in a closely knit pattern, tying numerous subordinates to his own principal, the pyramidal structure working together as a unit, a situation congenial to the objective person. This line organization strives for steady output and smooth operation. Advancement is prescribed and the objective man or woman moves steadily upward by progressive titles. In the textile industry these begin with second hand, in the factory with leading hand, gang boss, working foreman, subforeman, assistant foreman, and then still higher, department head, superintendent, through production manager, to general manager.

In contradistinction to this line organization, where the unique individual has no right to depart far from established policies, and expresses himself only within narrowly limited restrictions or by influencing the course of the entire structure, a staff member studies his own assignment, introduces revised practices, amends forms, plans new operations and factory layouts, duties which cut across the organization chart. He goes freely into any department, and succeeds or fails as an individual, a challenge to extreme subjectivity. Staff members work many years with no apparent promotion, climb no blazed trail. This often misleads extremely subjective workers into accepting a line position with a title, which they continue to hold, for the extremely subjective person does not ordinarily advance in the line organization. The same subjective person, continuing in the staff and doing brilliant work, may finally be appointed vice-president in charge of his own specialty without having previously mounted in title.

While the extremely subjective person does not naturally belong in business, he occasionally finds himself too well ensconced to withdraw, too old to go back to art, music, or research science. Like his sons, ages ten and thirteen, the assistant manager of an oil refinery, who made his test appointment solely to contribute genetic data, scored extremely subjective, a single significant response on worksample 35 form AE, none on form FC. He was an established executive with merited responsibility for the continuous operation of a highly technical plant, and doubted in consequence not only his own worksample scores but the advice to his sons. When the second half of his double appointment drew to a close, he analyzed himself more freely. As he came to know his business associates, he enjoyed them thoroughly; but he dreaded meeting strangers. For this reason, he knew at heart that he might be passed over in the next managerial appointment; the present incumbent, a non-technical man, handled community relations, customer goodwill, and the renewal of labor-union contracts, spending half his time away from the plant, work for which aptitude tests showed the present assistant manager inherently unfit. Yet, until tested, he had hoped to imitate exactly his predecessor.

Having just finished the testing of eighty executives for a manufacturing organization of three thousand employees, where the president scored extremely subjective, the Laboratory knew that a successful major executive might concern himself with operation problems, leaving labor relations and customer contacts to some gifted assistant. In this instance an executive vice-president who showed the ideal group-influencing pattern, high ideaphoria, extreme objectivity, and low structural visualization, handled all labor relationships with suave smoothness. Before his test the extremely subjective oil-plant assistant manager spent so much time preparing for the social mantle of his convivial superior that in technical knowledge he scored below where he should. His future lay in preparing, not to imitate, but to become an outstanding manager in charge of practical operations and simultaneously in developing a group-influencing assistant.

After four successful years in wholesale merchandizing, a heavy, dark-skinned salesman resented his extremely subjective score and wasted time rebelling at the outcome instead of facing impersonally the three alternatives to every aptitude finding. The test score may have been wrong; or, second, he may have succeeded because of other sales traits: high idea-phoria, low structural visualization, and average accounting aptitude; or, third, he may not have belonged in sales.

In this case a single objective response on two hundred items of worksample 35, composed of extreme scores on two forms, no significant response on form AE and one only on form FC, leaves but scant margin of doubt. Investigating the second alternative, the man scored low in ideaphoria, below the 15th percentile, and high in structural visualization, above the 80th. It is not, then, through other traits that he sells, and one must turn to the chance that, despite success, he belongs elsewhere.

Some sort of mechanical engineering offers this platoon of aptitudes a deeper satisfaction than either sales or advertising. Though he came to see if test scores substantiated manufacturing engineering, he interpreted his engineering aptitudes as reflecting on his sales ability and argued for an incessant quarter of an hour that he enjoyed selling, and prospered.

Two weeks later, after reading the brochure STRUCTURAL VISUALIZATION, he returned, still voluble over subjectivity, but reviewed quietly his home background. He early imitated the assured mannerisms of a successful executive father; but when he later inherited the family concern, it demanded more continuous selling than he enjoyed. After amusing himself with an income gained through liquidating the business, he turned to selling advertising. It needed no trained observer to sense his abnormal tenseness, an outward sign of uncongenial work, displayed by his instant scattering of the wiggly blocks with a nervous sweep and then asking what to do.

Like theatrical trappings and army uniforms, the panoply of business, seen from a distance, mesmerizes the subjective person. A university professor, son of a day laborer, rose in collegiate rank and during a long life earned an adequate if not luxurious stipend; but he overrode his son's infatuation for the Romance languages and sent him, after college, to an excellent business school, expecting to prepare him for practical life. Twelve years later, at the age of thirty-five, still doing routine clerical work at a lower salary than his father received at the same age, the son came to be tested with every aptitude of the born teacher of languages, table VII.

Although once the Laboratory felt keenly the mundane hardships of extreme subjectivity in a predominantly objective world, now it knows that the yearly earnings of objective business executives average no higher than those of skilled professionals, who achieve compensating happiness in their

TABLE VII

APTITUDES SUGGEST TEACHING

high	ideaphoria
high	inductive reasoning
high	abstract visualization
extremely subjective	personality
average	accounting aptitude
low	observation
low	structural visualization
very high	English vocabulary

APTITUDE SCORES CONFIRM THIS BOY'S INSTINCTIVE AMBITION TO TEACH A ROMANCE LANGUAGE; BUT, TO GRATIFY HIS FATHER, HE WENT TO BUSINESS SCHOOL AND LATER BECAME AN UNHAPPY MEDIOCRE ROUTINE CLERK, INSTEAD OF THE AFFLUENT AND INFLUENTIAL BANK PRESIDENT THE FATHER FORESAW.

intimate contributions to human welfare. In a group of college students tested in 1929, and personally interviewed in 1942, where approximately half turned toward some phase of business, and half followed professional engineering, the top third of the extremely subjective technicians earned exactly as much as the top third of the administrators. Discounting the objective multitude of subforemen, gang bosses, and petty officials, few of whom reach eminence, parents imagine every ambitious boy mounting steadily in business; but in the professional world they foresee the hardships with exaggerated clarity. A universal tendency contrasts the corporation president with the underpaid technician, the struggling musician, or the mediocre artist, magnifying the monetary returns of business. High earnings anywhere demand obdurate exertion.

Reckless devotion to business builds an impersonal organization, but not the enduring happiness of the extremely subjective person. After twenty years as treasurer of a small pencil company, an extremely subjective woman found herself unemployed at the age of fifty-three when the organization to which she had given her life was unexpectedly bought by a national group. Objective officers of lower rank received stock in the combined enterprise and positions for themselves, but she gave herself so unstintingly that she spared no thought to her own future. By contrast, years in medicine, law, or literary writing, long hours at the piano, or days at the easel, build an enviable reputation which guarantees old-age comfort.

More like high-school children in their enthusiasms than adults of thirty-three and thirty-two respectively, an extremely subjective couple wondered if they could start a diminutive business of their own, to be independent of the contending world. Both scored high in accounting aptitude, the wife at the 100th percentile, the husband at the 65th. After twelve years as a bank teller, he detested figures. In contrast with an objective person, who enjoys his daily job, who waits dispassionately on one client after another in a restless queue until his task is done, this extremely subjective man dreaded rush hours, with impatient humanity lined at his window, worried about the future, sought a final solution, a lasting contribution.

To the wife's proposal of raising flowers, and running a greenhouse, extremely subjective men and women are happier in control of their own time, directing their own efforts, and this wistful couple will undoubtedly enjoy hard labor toward a distant goal. But scientific horticulture, if it does not demand, can at least use structural visualization, where both husband and wife score low. Two extremely subjective humans attain real happiness only at the tops of their callings, and without structural visualization have little chance of fancying technical hothouse control or plant breeding.

Both score high in accounting aptitude and should handle well the finances of any undertaking, a point in favor of the wife's suggestion. Yet because raising flowers, and operating a greenhouse, becomes a business, and extreme subjectivity rarely expands in the routine handling of an established enterprise, and because low structural visualization will keep them from enjoying research into enzymes, soil chemistry, or cross fertilization, their horticultural project seems questionable.

Extremely subjective persons should lay the basis in their thirties for assured security at fifty. Running a profitable greenhouse, and raising flowers for a competitive market, means hard physical labor, difficult to continue as one grows older, or it means developing, installing, and operating, highly mechanical

TABLE VIII

APTITUDES SUGGEST NEWSPAPER REPORTING
ON FINANCIAL MATTERS

extremely subjective	in personality
(3 significant responses; form AE)	
high (100th percentile)	in accounting aptitude
high (95th percentile)	in observation
high (90th percentile)	in visual imagination
high (85th percentile)	in ideaphoria
high (80th percentile)	in abstract visualization
low (21st percentile)	in structural visualization

THIS WOMAN'S VISUAL IMAGINATION DEMANDED THAT SHE SEE A FUTURE MORE SATISFYING TO HERSELF THAN SECRETARIAL WORK. CERTIFIED PUBLIC ACCOUNTING WOULD USE HER ACCOUNTING APTITUDE, EXTREME SUBJECTIVITY, AND ABSTRACT VISUALIZATION, BUT NOT HER IDEAPHORIA.

scientific equipment, dependent upon structural visualization, or it means hiring and handling able-bodied helpers, an approach congenial to objective employers, or it means clever selling, again dependent on objectivity.

The wife, table VIII, began in secretarial work with a little chemical company and, in the intimacy of a small group, delved into planning sales campaigns and writing advertising copy, which used her creative imagination. Later she shifted to a larger organization. and then on to one still larger, always with greater responsibilities, but also more restricted. Finally at the age of thirty-two she realized that secretarial work promised her no ultimate satisfaction. Certified public accounting would use her extreme subjectivity, abstract visualization, and high accounting aptitude, but not her ideaphoria or observation. Creative writing would use everything she possesses except her 100th-percentile accounting aptitude. Realizing that writing should be a major activity the Laboratory felt that she should start instantly putting in the same long hours and hard work she had planned to devote to horticulture. One expects to pick prize flowers for the early market at five in the morning, and then to spray, prune, and cultivate, twelve hours more; but few amateurs regard writing as calling for similar effort. In addition she might study accounting, banking methods, international finance, to use her accounting aptitude, with the thought ultimately of writing on finance; although this might take more inductive reasoning and less ideaphoria than she possesses. As interviewing demands ideaphoria and virtually no inductive reasoning, reporting on the financial world approaches a solution of her problem, but could hardly use 100th-percentile accounting aptitude. Statistics is more likely than accounting to give ingress to some such field as public health on which again she might write. The capitalization of such an aptitude pattern toward a single unified goal is a full life's work.

In reaction to writing, parents comment that an ordinary boy survives in business, while literature, music, and the professions, reward only the genius, a contention not supported by unprejudiced study. In the twelve-year follow-up of two hundred men, the bottom third of the professional engineers averaged financially as much as the bottom third of the executives. If, as seems likely, three-quarters of mankind belong in objective pursuits, and only one-quarter in the extremely subjective arts and sciences, the chance of a misfit in these last is greater than in business, and one should expect more failures. Expressed crudely, there is only one chance in four of the wrong person's entering the business world; but three chances in four of the wrong one entering the fine arts. Also the arts are undoubtedly emotional, so that mediocrity seems more reprehensible. But failure in business affects the extremely subjective person as much as failure in art or music, for temperamental delicacy goes with this section of the personality scale, not with the occupation.

Contrasting with a carefree enjoyment of daily life. a casual criticism acutely wounds the extremely subjective person, silently scarred by some thoughtless remark or stray glance, an exaggerated susceptibility which affects the entire group from the great artist and eminent musician to the timekeeper for a steel construction company who declared that each day opened old wounds or brought fresh ones, and who could not understand how other men work oblivious to unmerited criticism, happy in the week's output, and not worrying about the future. Unless recognized for what it is, the inevitable result of living in a primarily objective world, this extreme sensitivity is one of the factors which helps to frame the setting for a nervous collapse.

Sensing his imminent exposure to hurt, the extremely subjective person often creates his own defeat. The elder son of a western manufacturer insisted upon direct selling. With boundless opportunities to turn wherever he wished, this gifted man elected the one distasteful task for which extreme subjectivity and high structural visualization least equipped him. When questioned, he admitted that he could not sell but wanted to conquer an imaginary weakness. His father's manufacturing organization needed his aptitude pattern in technical engineering; but extreme subjectivity drove him toward daily peddling because he regarded it as the rougher road.

One who craves the spiritual gratification of an unsuitable path can make the right road hard by tightening his standards of accomplishment; for titanic problems which so far defy the most gifted mortals stud every direction. At his death, this man's father left his fabricating business to a younger son, for both the family and the world viewed the subjective salesman as an incompetent failure; had he attacked a gigantic task befitting his extraordinary aptitudes, the world would marvel at the slightest progress. This man subconsciously condoned his failure by assuring himself that he could have succeeded elsewhere; the inappropriate road offers personal escape from disheartening actuality. Obedience to his aptitudes would have left him no excuse.

An extremely subjective boy, high in analytical reasoning, low in accounting aptitude, low in structural visualization, and at the 92nd percentile in vocabulary, anatomized himself with brutal incisiveness. Because of his low accounting aptitude and high vocabulary, the Laboratory recommended a small but old and academic college. The boy called all such ancient institutions stuffy, high brow. He hated formality. He liked the boundless out-of-doors and was an apathetic sophomore in a small, country preparatory school of thirty boys. He delighted in wasting time and squandered a whole year building a bookcase of two shelves which, he said, was not very good when finished. Then thoughtfully, with no prompting, he continued: " I think I see what you mean. My extremely subjective personality makes me enjoy feeling superior. In my low-vocabulary school, the boys ask me childish words, and marvel at my knowing them, while I wander around, looking at the way people live, and yet do the school work easily. You want me to work. But," he added after a moment's hesitation, " I would be afraid to challenge myself. I might fail."

In contradistinction to total individuality, that narrow segment tapped by worksample 35, which the Laboratory designates as PERSONALITY, the contrast between the objective person and the extremely subjective, does not change with hastening age and accumulating experience. For the scientifically minded reader, to whom induction appeals, here are technical reasons for accepting such unalterability.

CAN EXTREME SUBJECTIVITY BE CHANGED?

First, growing boys measured twice, with a lapse of years between, change little more in worksample 35 than between two forms in a double appointment. Were each determination accurate, two percentiles should of course be identical; but even with the high reliability of 0.92 to 0.95 separately determined ratings for an individual occasionally range widely. When this happens in a second appointment several years after the first even staff members wonder if it does not reflect intervening experience; but it occurs almost equally often with two forms a few days apart. It shows therefore an inaccuracy of the measuring instrument, not a change in personality.

Second, the similarity of distribution curves for different ages shows that the percentage of extremely subjective persons remains constant. Average scores in worksample 35 do not fluctuate; after about the twelfth year, boys of each age score the same as grown men. If extremely subjective persons become objective as they mature, or if degree of subjectivity changes with experience, adults should differ from children; personality should not remain fixed. An alternative inference, that for every boy who becomes objective with the years another becomes equally subjective, leaving the distribution curve and the mathematical average unchanged while individuals move about, seems unlikely. Life's experiences do not apparently shift the trait consistently in one direction or the other.

Third, and more intangible, the bimodal distribution with a gap at the quarter fits the assumption of a discontinuous inherited factor. With our present knowledge, the wisest course seems to be an acceptance of extreme subjectivity as a fixed, immutable, unitary characteristic.

Expressed sketchily, and circumventing all cautious qualifications, inherited traits descend through the generations by means of genes. These occur in pairs. Two dominant genes produce the dominant trait; two recessive genes, the recessive trait; while a pair composed of a dominant and of a recessive gene together produce the dominant appearance. There are exceptions; but either because research gradually uncovers an intrinsically simple universal plan or because man insists upon arranging facts so that he remembers them easily, nature displays a surprising organization as scientists penetrate its mysteries. In general the less complicated an assumption the more likely is it to survive coming centuries. Punctilious technicians make measurements which temporarily fail to fit, and so elaborate; and once started the process ramifies, until a later generation regroups the entire network into nearly the original plan. The Laboratory assumes that extreme subjectivity results from a recessive gene which occurs about half the time, with approximately a fifty per cent frequency, and that in consequence the recessive phenotype, the outward appearance resulting from a pair of recessive genes, occurs in one-quarter of the population.

The distribution of form AE should resemble figure 1; three-quarters of examinees identical at about 22 significant responses, and one-quarter near 2. But inaccuracies in the measuring instrument cause dispersion about these theoretical values; for even in the exact sciences technicians vary in estimating the

FIGURE I

THEORETICAL DISTRIBUTION OF PERSONALITY
WITH A PERFECT MEASURING INSTRUMENT

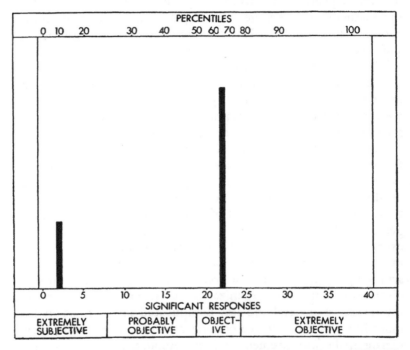

THIS FIGURE SHOWS THREE-QUARTERS OF ALL PERSONS SCORING AT 22 SIGNIFICANT
RESPONSES, AND ONE-QUARTER AT 2, A DISTRIBUTION WHICH THE LABORATORY
BELIEVES WILL BE APPROACHED AS THE ACCURACY OF WORKSAMPLE 35 GRADU-
ALLY IMPROVES THROUGH FURTHER RESEARCH.

last decimal, fail to hold temperature and pressure immovable.
Plotted horizontally, from left to right, heterogeneous errors
give a so-called normal or Gaussian curve rising near the
theoretically correct value at the center and tapering off
laterally. When applied to the word-association test, worksample 35 form AE, objective persons do not fall at exactly
22 significant responses but scatter, one in a thousand giving
thirty-eight and one in a thousand five or less, as represented
by the bell-shaped curve at the right of figure 2. A similar

FIGURE 2

THEORETICAL DISTRIBUTION OF PERSONALITY
WITH AN INACCURATE MEASURING INSTRUMENT

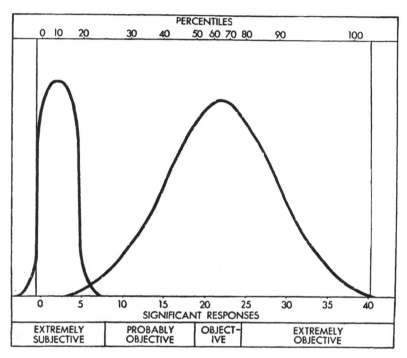

THIS FIGURE SHOWS THE NORMAL CURVE OF ERRORS DRAWN AROUND THE TWO
THEORETICAL POINTS, 2 AND 22 SIGNIFICANT RESPONSES, IN SUCH A WAY THAT
THE AREA UNDER THE RIGHT-HAND CURVE IS THREE TIMES THE OTHER.

curve represents errors of measurement from the theoretical
figure of two significant responses given by the extremely subjective person, inaccuracies ranging by the law of chance from
zero to six or seven. Figure 3 shows these theoretical curves
superimposed on the existent distribution.

The right-hand curve fits well, the left not so closely; but
a recent discovery by Marie H. Licht, relating to blocked responses, seems to indicate that with the next step toward greater
accuracy will come a materially closer fit of the theoretical
curve to the low scores, which now pile up at zero.

FIGURE 3

FIGURE 3

THEORETICAL DISTRIBUTION OF PERSONALITY
SUPERIMPOSED ON THE ACTUAL DISTRIBUTION

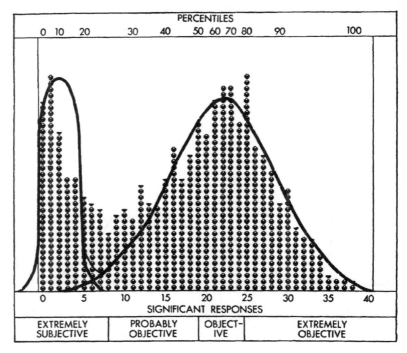

EACH HALF DOT REPRESENTS THE SCORE OF SOMEONE ACTUALLY MEASURED WITH WORKSAMPLE 35 FORM AE, A TOTAL OF 1420 ADULT MEN. THE SUPER-IMPOSED THEORETICAL CURVES ARE REPRODUCED FROM FIGURE 2.

An examinee at four or five significant responses is presumably extremely subjective, but may be objective, belonging at 22 significant responses but scoring below because of discrepancies in the measuring instrument. Statistically rare, this occurrence is vital for the individual to whom it happens. Recognition of the objective person who scores below eight responses comes with the administration of a second form, or sometimes a third, a year later. This means that occasionally a man scores extremely subjective on one form and objective on others, an average of all giving the soundest indication.

During his first session a quietly assured advertising executive scored twelve significant responses on form AE, in the section then called SUBJECTIVE, now PROBABLY OBJECTIVE. Granted that theoretically any score between eight and forty counts as objective, one cannot help questioning a borderline case especially with a quiet man. In the second half of his double appointment he scored 20 significant responses on form FJ, a total of 32 on the combination, unmistakably objective, the type of personality which corresponds with his success in advertising.

PROBABLY OBJECTIVE

EXTREME SUBJECTIVITY on independent forms, zero to 8 on form AE, and zero to 5 on form FJ, figure 4, average unchallenged EXTREMELY SUBJECTIVE on the combination. But not every extremely subjective person on one form scores equally subjective on the other. An examinee may score 12 on form AE, in the PROBABLY OBJECTIVE quarter, and only 5 on form FJ, EXTREMELY SUBJECTIVE, a total of 17. Another may score 9 on form AE, and 6 on form FJ, both PROBABLY OBJECTIVE for the separate forms, but adding to only 15. To compare these final scores the Laboratory plots a fresh distribution curve based on the sum of forms AE and FJ, and published as the frontispiece to IDEAPHORIA. This shows that one quarter of examinees score 18 or less on the sum of these two forms. A score of 10 significant responses on form AE, called PROBABLY OBJECTIVE, with 8 on form FJ, again PROBABLY OBJECTIVE on this form alone, add to 18, which on the combined scale falls in the EXTREMELY SUBJECTIVE quarter. PROBABLY OBJECTIVE scores on two separate forms, and EXTREME SUBJECTIVITY on the combination, annoys everyone whose scores combine in this quizzical manner.

The reason for labeling a quarter of the combined scores as EXTREMELY SUBJECTIVE is the same as that for the separate forms, the shape of the distribution curve. With every test the rudimentary tentative assumption is a line at the center; but a bimodal curve as unmistakable as figure 1, page 14, of UNSOLVED BUSINESS PROBLEMS, showing the distribution of 1420 adult males for form AE, forces one to accept the valley between the peaks as the natural division between two types of persons. This comes at the quarter, at the 25th percentile,

FIGURE 4

DISTRIBUTION OF PERSONALITY MEASURED BY
WORKSAMPLE 35 FORM FJ

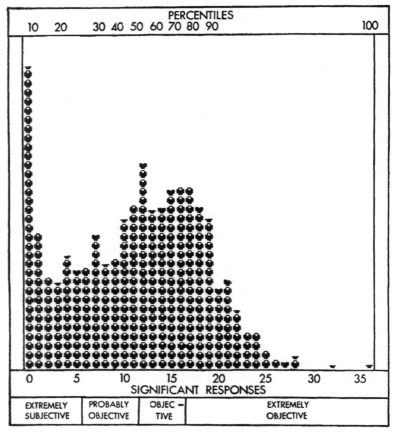

THIS FIGURE SHOWS THE DISTRIBUTION OF SCORES MADE BY 1091 PERSONS. AP-
PROXIMATELY ONE QUARTER. 25 PER CENT. GIVE FIVE OR FEWER SO-CALLED SIG-
NIFICANT RESPONSES. THREE QUARTERS, CALLED OBJECTIVE, GIVE SIX OR MORE.

with form AE. With the newer form FJ the gap is not so clear;
but with the combination it comes again near the quarter. For
form AE it occurs between 7 and 8 significant responses; for
form FJ, between 5 and 6 significant responses; and for forms
AE plus FJ at a point between 18 and 19 significant responses.

For insurance against inaccuracies one who scores within ten percentiles of the critical point at the twenty-fifth should not gamble too much on the finding. The Laboratory works incessantly to better the accuracy of its measuring instruments; but no result is ever infallible. In physics and chemistry an error means little more than a waste of experimental time, for more measurements can be taken and the truth gradually attained; but in psychometrics each measurement is a human being. Statistically the Laboratory is right; but each person tested must realize that in his or her own case the indications may be wrong by ten percentiles or more. For everyone in this doubtful region, from the 15th to the 35th percentile, between four and twelve significant responses on form AE, the wise policy is to assume extreme subjectivity. In those cases where the test is correct the really objective person can often afford to act subjectively without undue harm. The extremely subjective person who by mistake supposes himself objective and behaves accordingly becomes too blatantly the stentorian back-slapper and blusters into awkward social situations.

In writing these interpretive brochures, the author plans some for objective persons, others for the extremely subjective, some for those high in structural visualization, others for those who score low. Thus UNSOLVED BUSINESS PROBLEMS treats of the combination low structural visualization and objectivity, two basic executive traits. STRUCTURAL VISUALIZATION, as the title implies, discusses this engineering aptitude linked with objectivity. APTITUDES AND THE LANGUAGES deals with abstract visualization, revealed by a low score in the structural tests; while IDEAPHORIA includes the aptitude formerly called CREATIVE IMAGINATION, together with objectivity and low structural visualization. The test administrator, who must select a suitable volume at the close of an appointment, fits every person into one of these arbitrary categories. But for many examinees this is not the wise approach to a practical interpretation of a worksample pattern.

A ninth-grade boy scored four significant responses on worksample 35 form AE, in the extremely subjective division, but PROBABLY OBJECTIVE on form FJ, averaging exactly at the critical line, a result which the staff often wrongly calls BORDER-

LINE PERSONALITY. To help decide between the applicability of an objective or extremely subjective brochure, one argues that form AE is better understood, more exhaustively analyzed, and should in consequence be weighted, throwing the combined score into the extremely subjective quarter. But acknowledged

TABLE IX

APTITUDES WHICH SUGGEST WRITING

high (90th percentile)	abstract visualization
high (90th percentile)	ideaphoria
high (80th percentile)	inductive reasoning
low (11th percentile)	structural visualization
low (5th percentile)	accounting aptitude
low (10th percentile)	English vocabulary

THE MEASURED PERSONALITY OF THIS BOY IS DOUBTFUL AND SHOULD BE IGNORED IN THE INTERPRETATION OF HIS APTITUDE PATTERN. HE BELONGS IN WRITING; IF OBJECTIVE HE WILL FIND A COMFORTABLE EDITORIAL CHAIR, IF EXTREMELY SUBJECTIVE HE WILL RUN A PERSONAL COLUMN OR DO FREE-LANCE WORK.

inaccuracies of the measuring instrument still leave the mean score too near the critical point. It is sounder to build first around other aptitudes, where measurements are not in question. This boy scores as shown in table IX, the unmistakable pattern of the writer. For many years he can go confidently toward creative writing without troubling about his personality. If objective he will gravitate toward editorial supervision, if extremely subjective toward free-lance writing; both require that he improve his English vocabulary from its present low, 10th-percentile level to the 80th or above, a long, hard, ten years' endeavor. While designed specifically for the extremely subjective person, this brochure is occasionally given to one who scores probably objective, either because of other traits, or because the examinee has taken only one personality form and may score extremely subjective on a second.

In reasoning from the composite scores of successful men to the probable future of an inexperienced youth, one must avoid an obscure pitfall. Artists, musicians, writers, laboratory technicians, research scientists, and skilled surgeons, average extremely subjective; and the untried boy who scores in this section should investigate these prototypes. Salesmen and advertisers average extremely objective, and the boy or girl at the opposite end should ordinarily turn elsewhere. Extending this same reasoning, one is tempted to conclude that, because professional men and women average PROBABLY OBJECTIVE, a boy or girl should score in this part of the scale to enter a profession. This does not follow; if true it would indicate different futures for those who score PROBABLY OBJECTIVE, OBJECTIVE, and EXTREMELY OBJECTIVE, and other evidence indicates no fundamental difference between these types, variations in test score resulting from extraneous factors.

An explanation which fits all facts is that so large a percentage of artists, scientists, and surgeons, are extremely subjective that the group as a whole average in this part of the scoring scale; similarly, an overwhelming majority of salesmen are objective. But in the professions there are both objective and extremely subjective persons; and because the latter predominate the group average toward the subjective end, in the section now called PROBABLY OBJECTIVE.

Among thirty experienced graduate nurses from the top of the profession, nearly half, those in private duty, score extremely subjective, while the reverse half, those in executive positions, score objective or extremely objective. The group averages PROBABLY OBJECTIVE, between these extremes, but not one actual person chances to score in this mid section.

Each extremely subjective person sails his own unique course, for, even in the word-association test, extreme subjectivity is not a type. To the stimulus: MUSIC, one hundred and eighty persons in every thousand answer PIANO and at one time this response counted 180 points toward the final score; to the same word, twenty-one others answer VIOLIN, and this counted 21. Later, in a revised method, the research department awarded one point for a most common answer, one for PIANO and nothing for any other reaction to MUSIC. Both methods rest on commonality, both select approximately those called OBJECTIVE. The present system, a third refinement, is based on responses picked statistically

UNIQUE
COURSE

because they are given consistently by objective men and women and not by subjective. In repeated analyses, the research department fails to locate a single response characteristic of extreme subjectivity; nothing typifies this end of the scoring scale except the absence of its opposite.

Much as a subjective score on the word-association test depends upon an absence of objective responses, and not a direct count of subjective ones, so advice to the subjective person counsels the avoidance of hackneyed, clearly typical, objective jobs. The extremely subjective man or woman should eliminate from consideration the banal business world. If low in structural visualization, he should next set architecture aside, as well as structural engineering and surgery; if low in accounting aptitude, banking and accounting should follow; for one who scores extremely subjective is too unusual a person to fit a limited pattern and should instead seek the unique course, reaching fresh work by drastic pruning.

The present brochure might describe OBJECTIVITY, followed by the statement: this is not SUBJECTIVITY. One attracted by this scientifically sound, antithetical approach should THE UNIQUE read the four previous brochures: UNSOLVED INDIVIDUAL BUSINESS PROBLEMS, THE TOO-MANY-APTITUDE WOMAN, STRUCTURAL VISUALIZATION, and IDEAPHORIA, all designed for objectivity. This brochure describes numerous extremely subjective individuals and their unique experiences, hoping to give the subjective reader inspiration from actual illustrations and corresponding insight into himself.

II

ACCOUNTING APTITUDE

With the myopic sanction of sympathetic teachers and parents, typical low-accounting-aptitude pupils substitute French for the bothersome Latin, and though advanced education no longer calls for an ancient language discover four years later, to their enduring chagrin, that this shortsighted decision cost entrance to the college of their choice; for, despite a brief deceptive interval, the regrettable step from Latin soon lowers school marks. Its easy abandonment gives a boy immediate surplus time, which for a few days he spends on other lessons; and then the same low accounting aptitude makes the remaining subjects equally hard and he does no more than formerly.

Latin underlies an intelligent grasp of English vocabulary, and this in turn correlates with academic performance. When English vocabulary ceases to grow at its former rate all schooling becomes progressively laborious, and with the same total effort a boy obtains lower marks. Latin is trying and one who turns aside rationalizes the indulgent acceptance of the easy road. French is next discarded and replaced by the simpler Spanish. Later the college registrar, who deals with enough cases to recognize instinctively the indolent boy, sees no Latin, no French, and though his own college catalogue accepts Spanish he rejects the remiss applicant.

For lack of language credits, boys low in accounting aptitude forsake the Bachelor of Arts degree for the Bachelor of Science, in the mistaken belief that the distinction is now negligible. Then arithmetic bores them; and they transfer their clerical ineptitude to a sluggish aversion for all mathematics, forgetting their real enjoyment in analyzing an illusive problem. This leaves them incapable of science; and they shift from the college-preparatory program often by exclusion to a so-called business or commercial course in a vocational school, which seems practical but is in reality the worse direction for the poor clerk and which leads low-accounting-aptitude boys and girls toward unsuitable jobs where their chances are nine to one of remaining in the bottom quarter of the country's earnings, for low accounting aptitude pushes eager boys and girls relentlessly from the remote goal which might embrace their strong propensities. The effective solution stops this chain of irreversible steps at the outset, with persistence in Latin no matter how tedious.

The enchanting son of a restaurant waiter, an extremely subjective boy, in mid-ninth grade, studying bookkeeping in a New York commercial high school, produced the aptitude pattern of the editorial writer, table x. Comments from his youthful pen had already appeared in the school paper; but athletics preoccupied his leisure. At age fourteen insistence on writing would prejudice him irrevocably; but he should not miss early essential background, though he might not appreciate its purport. Yet exactly this happens to countless low-accounting-aptitude boys whose parents expect their sons to

TABLE X

APTITUDES WHICH SUGGEST EDITORIAL WRITING

high (95th percentile)	inductive reasoning
high (95th percentile)	abstract visualization
average (70th percentile)	ideaphoria
average (70th percentile)	observation
low (15th percentile)	accounting aptitude

BECAUSE OF VERY LOW ACCOUNTING APTITUDE, THIS HIGH-SCHOOL BOY WAS FORCED TO DROP ALL LANGUAGES AND TO SHIFT TO THE COMMERCIAL, BOOK-KEEPING COURSE. AT AGE 14 HE HAS BEEN CUT OFF FROM ALL CHANCE OF GETTING THE ACADEMIC BACKGROUND ESSENTIAL TO HIS APTITUDES.

earn a moderate sustenance at ordinary levels. With no social position to uphold, the average low-accounting-aptitude boy, overwhelmed by school troubles, handicapped in all written work, including the usual high-speed, paper-and-pencil, general intelligence test, sees little object in striving for classical languages and so retreats to the lower academic standards of the commercial course. Later his own future ostensibly justifies this favored policy, for he takes a minor clerical job, where his 15th percentile accounting aptitude leads to a plodding life of clerical drudgery, or to rebellion against a social order which gives him no chance to use the born gifts he feels within, and so from a worldly viewpoint seems to prove that he was always mediocre. The Laboratory believes that every extremely subjective boy, low in structural visualization and low in accounting aptitude, should persevere with the academic, college-preparatory course, including Latin. But many fathers and mothers lack the almost blind confidence, combined with social standing and political influence needed to save their low-accounting-aptitude sons from the general rule of shunting all with classroom troubles to low-standard vocational courses.

FIGURE 5

ACCOUNTING APTITUDE OF ADULT MEN
AS MEASURED BY
NUMBER CHECKING WORKSAMPLE 268

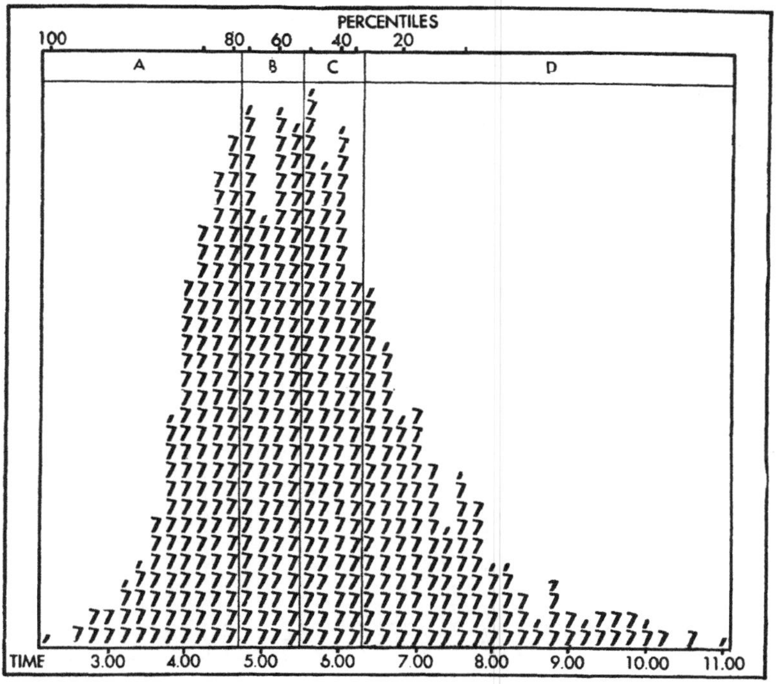

THIS DISTRIBUTION CURVE SHOWS THE TOTAL TIME IN MINUTES USED IN CHECK-
ING FIVE SHEETS, RANGING FROM FOUR DIGITS TO EIGHT, IGNORING THE FIRST
THREE-DIGIT SHEET REGARDED AS PRACTICE. THE CURVE IS BASED ON 945 ADULT
MEN, EACH SYMBOL REPRESENTING TWO.

Almost every low-accounting-aptitude person makes careless
clerical mistakes, and in consequence both parents and teachers
urge more pains; but slowing down does not help. On the
number-checking tests, worksamples 1 and 268, fast examinees
are statistically slightly more accurate than slow ones. The
correspondence is not close and in consequence not obvious
to the lay world; but despite the familiar adage, slow workers
are not accurate, nor do they lower their errors by lagging.

FIGURE 6

Accounting Aptitude of Adult Women
as measured by
Number Checking Worksample 268

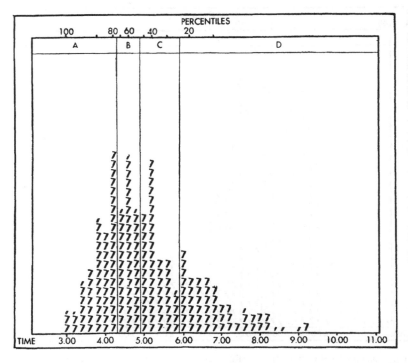

THIS DISTRIBUTION CURVE IS BASED ON 420 ADULT WOMEN. WORKSAMPLE 268 IS A PURER AND MORE ACCURATE INDICATION OF ACCOUNTING APTITUDE THAN THE ORIGINAL WORKSAMPLE I.

One who speeds ahead does not instantly gain the inward satisfaction of reduced errors; permanently improved accuracy develops only with continued repetition. To achieve clerical experience, the low-accounting-aptitude student must rush through every clerical operation; for the faster he performs a task the more often can he repeat it. Although diametrically opposed to parental warnings, this iconoclastic advice rests on controlled Laboratory measurements. With each repetition comes greater speed, and ultimately fewer errors. The pedagogic fear, that mistakes form a careless habit, is not borne out by measurements. With each repetition comes greater accuracy; but with errors do not come more errors.

In addition the hesitant, low-accounting-aptitude pupil, who knows by experience that he makes mistakes, and tends stolidly to chainstitch, must habituate himself to finishing each clerical task before checking, otherwise the benefits of practice never accrue. The timid boy who does correctly one algebra problem out of ten, or one Latin sentence, obtains a school mark of ten per cent, one tenth of a hundred; and passes no course. Could the same boy finish each problem more quickly, getting only half right, he would grade fifty per cent on the lesson and with but slight additional effort could correct enough errors to raise his mark to passing. But he must not start looking for errors until he has completed the lesson; otherwise he spends more time than he realizes in checking.

The low-accounting-aptitude boy writes down laboriously the first few steps in the solution of some mathematical problem; and then suddenly his unrestrained thinking races inadvertently ahead, omitting equations accurately thought through but too quickly to record. Holding back a boy's mental growth to his clerical speed is not the answer; for every unused aptitude brings on symptoms remarkably like those shown by the left-eyed examinee who uses his right hand, tenseness, nervousness, restlessness, even speech difficulties. The low-accounting-aptitude examinee must drive his pencil to keep up with his fastest aptitude. Even if this led to egregious inaccuracy the Laboratory would still believe it a farsighted procedure. Fortunately it results in fewer errors, not more; and there are both accuracy and therapy back of the advice.

The low-accounting-aptitude boy lightens his language assignments by the habit of translating with the text book closed. Ideal steps in a recommended procedure are:

(1) Read the daily lesson rapidly from beginning to end, including the accompanying vocabulary.

(2) Conceal from sight all but the allotted sentences, and translate these from Latin to English, or the reverse, without reference to the printed vocabulary and grammar. The student

may know only one or two words, may remember only a first letter, and be uncertain of each ending; but the important point is to write as much of every sentence as possible. One who follows this practice honestly, without cheating, without peeking to catch some half-remembered word, will find, perhaps to his amazement, that within a week or ten days he can write half the words and half the endings, grading fifty per cent. After finishing the entire lesson with this technique, a low-accounting-aptitude boy should read the lesson again, cover the text, and fill the remaining blanks. This ordinarily raises his mark to passing.

Too often a boy starts with the first sentence to be translated, and copies each word in turn from the vocabulary of the day, primarily a clerical routine which adds little to permanent knowledge and soon leaves one low in accounting aptitude irretrievably behind. The recommended procedure means that words, endings, syntax, and grammar, enter the boy's mind as he reads the lesson and come from it again as he writes the sentences, becoming in this way mental rather than clerical. The Laboratory finds no connection between clerical slowness and cerebral speed; so that a boy who scores low in accounting aptitude and high in any other aptitude, such as inductive reasoning, analytical reasoning, or number memory, should do every task mentally rather than clerically.

For one low in accounting aptitude, the small student body, with classes of five or less, is imperative. With thirty pupils in the same room, the average boy recites two minutes an hour, gaining trammeled expression only through documentary reports, a dangerous aggravation for one who thinks more rapidly than he writes.

Viewing a private school to meet his son's low accounting aptitude as financially impractical, a department-store executive enumerated four cogent reasons for public school, and called upon the Laboratory to weigh the counterbalancing factors. They were: first, an expensive private school imposes a grave financial burden; second, the father believed a naturally retiring boy should meet a democratic public; third, the boy thus far held his rightful academic place in public school; and, fourth, by further application he could build his vocabulary.

Four years earlier, when tested at age nine, then at the 24th percentile in English vocabulary, this shy boy was urged to improve, but had since fallen back to the 22nd percentile. The father countered that the boy had been too young to appreciate counsel; but the original notes asked both parents to help. The slight drop was undoubtedly a discrepancy of measurement; but expressed in bald figures it seemed unwise to continue where four years produced no gain.

In confirmation of the father's third point, the boy was thirteen, in eighth grade, and not retarded; but the mammoth high school, to be entered the next year, served five primary schools, and the low-accounting-aptitude boy seemed headed for inevitable trouble.

In refutation of the father's trust in a representative social environment, the extremely subjective child gains more community confidence through sound basic knowledge than through forced contact with the public.

The financial question the Laboratory cannot argue, presenting the desirability of a small school where feasible.

Neighboring towns, each with its own elementary group separately housed, or small primary schools scattered over a medium-sized city, customarily amalgamate into a single centralized high school, larger than the merging units, making the upward step from the elementary grades to the nearby but overwhelming high school calamitous for the low-accounting-aptitude boy who experienced no report troubles through eighth grade.

From an apprehensive mother in a small mid-western city came a querying letter wondering if caution of potential troubles might not precipitate them. In two years her extremely subjective son would enter the township high school, enormous by comparison; commute an hour each day, time which one low in accounting aptitude can ill afford; and compete with generally high-accounting-aptitude strangers drawn from contributing schools. In prospect, the shift seemed disastrous, for the boy needed the languages given by high school and college. Ideally, two years hence this sixth-grade boy should enroll in some small private preparatory school. The mother demurred but realized that if she waited until forced she might discourage the boy needlessly; and unless she planned ahead she would be financially impotent when the time came. She lost nothing by providence and two years later led a group of parents in organizing a small private school serving three neighboring cities.

APTITUDES AND THE LANGUAGES lists 246 preparatory boarding schools for boys, some starting at seventh grade, others at ninth, all continuing through twelfth, and ranging in size from a total of fifteen pupils to seven hundred and thirty. To reduce the fatiguing, nerve-racking, clerical routine a boy in the bottom quarter for his age in accounting aptitude belongs in a small school of not more than seventy pupils; individual attention in a large group is no substitute. For one who grades C in accounting aptitude, a preparatory school of seventy-five to one hundred and thirty pupils represents an effective size; while for one who grades B, the Laboratory recommends one hundred and forty to two hundred and forty pupils. Another boy who scores in the top quarter in accounting aptitude should challenge the trait in a large preparatory school of two hundred and fifty or more.

THE TOO-MANY-APTITUDE WOMAN lists colleges in similar fashion under three headings: technical institutes which admit girls and which the Laboratory recommends to those who grade A in structural visualization; coeducational colleges which give engineering degrees, and which the Laboratory recommends to girls who grade B in structural visualization; and finally women's colleges. Each of these three groups is subdivided into nine, three groups of large colleges for girls who rank high in accounting aptitude, three of intermediate size for those average, and three small ones for those low in accounting aptitude. STRUCTURAL VISUALIZATION lists corresponding technical institutes for men, coeducational colleges giving engineering degrees, and men's colleges.

Pages 177 to 193 of the present volume list 287 coeducational colleges, starting with 12 old, large ones which the Laboratory recommends to those who score high in both English vocabulary and accounting aptitude, going next to a group equally large but not so old, and therefore less academic, recommended to those who rate average in vocabulary but high in accounting aptitude; and ending with recently founded, small coeducational colleges where the Laboratory believes those gain most from their four years who rate low in English vocabulary and low in accounting aptitude.

Prejudiced parents embellish the social standing of a fashionable school, its policy of personal instruction, and all but force a staff member to approve. Countless factors influence selection: tuition, location, family connections, and tradition, renowned faculty members, special courses, date of foundation, as well as size in relation to accounting aptitude; but an unintentional perverting of the Laboratory's impersonal criteria under well-meant pressure leads often to tragic consequences. A morning mail brought two letters. At the first natural break after scoring low in accounting aptitude, at the termination of sophomore year in high school, Randy, described in the gratifying letter, transferred pleasantly to a small school. He had previously disliked study, rebelled against reading, and refused to plan on further education; in his new surroundings he began sending for college catalogues, and now, three years after his test appointment, he had just completed his college freshman work. The second letter, from another family, told of Sam who continued in the local public school of several hundred pupils, though he scored equally low in accounting aptitude. In the small city where they lived, his parents knew the high-school principal, and most of the teachers. Sam counted on continuing his father's legal practice; but after a fifth high-school year his father's college refused him admittance.

The Laboratory intends never to stress advice, for numerous factors, outside current understanding, affect human destinies. But it will soon test twenty thousand persons annually. Already nearly a hundred boys, previously tested and roughly comparable in accounting aptitude, enrolled in one college class, and set a common pace which others, who differed materially in accounting aptitude, failed to hold.

No matter what his aptitudes, almost no boy can plunge smoothly during a school year into a new chapter in a different text book, approaching a subject with altered emphasis. A fifteen-year-old youngster, in a coeducational school of one hundred and fifty pupils, the right size to challenge his 65th percentile accounting aptitude, recently founded and so not too academic for his low vocabulary, failed both algebra and Latin. In conference with the mother, the test administrator stated flatly that she saw no reason for classroom failure or even trouble. To a chance query at leave-taking, how long had the boy been in his present school, the mother replied: only four months; he shifted at mid-year from an old, academic, high-vocabulary institution. Transfer to a small school should await the end of an academic year.

The pathetic instances where financial restrictions render the small school impractical must be partially met by speeding up all clerical work, by completing every assignment rapidly to the end before attempting to check, and by a steady strengthening of English vocabulary. At their wit's end over the discouraging reports of an extremely subjective, low-accounting-aptitude, twelve-year-old boy, already cowed by disheartening school records, neither his hard-working mother, who supports herself and her son by scrubbing floors, nor his uncle, who owns a neighborhood fruit stand, can afford the luxury of a private school. Without the techniques which meet, though never overcome, low accounting aptitude, and without vocabulary, this boy must spend three or four times as long on home work as the average pupil; with vocabulary comes improved performance and a slightly better chance of entering ultimately one of the intellectual professions: law, college teaching, writing, historical research, called for by this boy's abstract visualization and extreme subjectivity, but glaringly absurd for anyone below the 5th vocabulary percentile.

The early struggle against low accounting aptitude meets many dispiriting obstacles. In the face of a sincere liking for an extremely subjective, eleven-year-old boy, not yet retarded, his sixth-grade, public-school teacher gradually lost patience with his enraging slovenliness, and warned that he might fail arithmetic. The mother helped and he improved. But soon she also applied the adjectives CARELESS and LAZY generally evoked by low accounting aptitude. Could both mother and teacher persevere, the boy scores high enough in other aptitudes to succeed in adult life, once over the school barrier; but if they give up he will forever lack formal preparation.

When a boy's aptitudes indicate a field which demands a sheepskin diploma, conscientious parents must do everything in their power to help gain this end. One who aspired to medical research and who resembled the microscopist in aptitudes, table XI, scored in addition:

high   in creative imagination, but
low (below 5th percentile) in accounting aptitude, and
equally low   in English vocabulary.

TABLE XI

TRAITS OF THE MICROSCOPIST

high   observation
high   structural visualization
high   tweezer dexterity
high   finger dexterity
extremely subjective   personality

THE IMPORTANCE OF OBSERVATION TO THE MICROSCOPIST IS OBVIOUS. STRUCTURAL VISUALIZATION HE USES IN BUILDING THE CONCEPT OF A SOLID OBJECT FROM A SERIES OF THIN SECTIONS. TWEEZER DEXTERITY, AND TO SOME EXTENT FINGER DEXTERITY, HE USES IN MOUNTING SPECIMENS AND CONSTRUCTING SLIDES, WHILE EXTREME SUBJECTIVITY IS THE PERSONALITY OF THE RESEARCH SCIENTIST.

Gifted with the inherent aptitudes for his keen ambition, but without the bookkeeping facility demanded by modern educational mills, he scores in consequence low in formal knowledge. By racking overwork, and after repeating a year, he graduated from high school and entered a medium-sized college where he led the class in laboratory work but failed every written test. On probation as a freshman, he left by request at the end of sophomore year. The despairing father saw no alternative but the last relinquishment of college, together with medical research; and aware that salesmen score objective in personality, as opposed to his son's extreme subjectivity, and low in structural visualization, in contrast to the boy's high score, he felt that under the unhappy circumstances his own insurance agency held the only future left, for the college president rejected reinstatement and averred no college in the country would admit so feeble a student. Pursuing its policy of never scrapping good material without a strenuous effort, the Laboratory persuaded the father to approach other colleges. With the directness of his own sales technique, he telephoned three, long distance, related to each the unvarnished story, and requested an appointment for his son to meet the registrar. The first one visited accepted the boy and the accompanying responsibilities. Though a dozen colleges turn away the low-accounting-aptitude boy, as may happen, parents should not rest content until they have tried the last one of the several hundred which are available.

The Laboratory's confidence in its own convictions comes frequently from testing a boy of fifteen, a man of thirty, and a third ten years older, with the same aptitudes, and by a study of the older man seeing the problems which the boy will meet. An extremely subjective man, making clerical tabulations of tariffs for the customs department of the United States government, was told by his colleagues and superiors that he should study accounting and law. Like professional accountants, he scores extremely subjective; but opposed to this practical advice, he scores at the 20th percentile in accounting aptitude, too low to gamble several years of exhausting study with slight chance of accounting success; also high in ideaphoria, at the 80th percentile, his top trait, where accountants score low; and above the median, 60th percentile, in structural visualization. For law the man shows inductive reasoning, 63d percentile, and extreme subjectivity; but this profession again would not tax his structural visualization.

The man spoke of aeronautical design as using structural visualization, ideaphoria, and his subjective personality; but this type of engineering is highly mathematical and sometimes laborious for one low in accounting aptitude. His favorite reading was archaeology and geology, either a perfect outlet for the man's complete pattern, which suggested a professional approach to creative work in a non-mathematical but structural field. Years earlier, in high school, he averaged ninety in his sciences, and did especially well in an introductory survey of geology; an evening course in accounting he dropped without finishing, he thought at the time for reasons other than inability, but now began to wonder.

By his own statement he held an assured position, where practical advancement demanded accounting and law. Remote, theoretical, almost fanciful, was an aptitude pattern which inferred geology and archaeology, fascinating subjects which he had never regarded as vocational possibilities. Reasonable steps

TABLE XII

APTITUDES USED IN ARCHAEOLOGY
AND GEOLOGICAL RESEARCH

extremely subjective	personality
high (80th percentile)	ideaphoria
average (63d percentile)	inductive reasoning
average (60th percentile)	structural visualization
low (20th percentile)	accounting aptitude

THIS CIVIL-SERVICE CLERK MADE ROUTINE TABULATIONS FOR THE FEDERAL GOVERNMENT IN WASHINGTON. ADVANCEMENT REQUIRED ACCOUNTING OR LAW. HE SCORES TOO LOW IN ACCOUNTING APTITUDE TO STUDY ACCOUNTING WITH REASONABLE CHANCE OF SUCCESS, AND IN LAW WOULD NOT USE HIS STRUCTURAL VISUALIZATION. WITHOUT LOSING HIS CIVIL-SERVICE RATING, HE MANAGED TO TRANSFER TO THE GEODETIC SURVEY, WHERE INTENSIVE STUDY OF GEOLOGY AND ARCHAEOLOGY SHOULD LEAD TO AN IDEAL FUTURE.

within reach were: First, buy used books on geology and archaeology until he possessed an extensive library, perhaps a thousand volumes. Second, take an evening course on geology in the local university. Third, apply for transfer to clerical work with the Geological Survey or the United States Weather Bureau, still on the government payroll, for he was doing little more than routine clerical work where he was.

Temporary expediencies turn hesitant men and women from sound goals not clearly fixed. An extremely subjective woman, who ten years later showed the aptitude pattern essential to law, started as private secretary for a legal counsellor. Then a salary raise induced her to supervise the filing of life insurance documents, which she continued for ten years. Tested at this point she scored:

high	in inductive reasoning,
low	in accounting aptitude, and
low	in English vocabulary.

The legal future she once pictured, which would use high inductive reasoning, meant turning back time's pages and doing at the age of thirty-five what should have been done earlier, building her vocabulary by academic courses in English composition, in history, in the languages, and subsequently or simultaneously starting the evening study of law itself.

In conformity with her inherent pattern, low accounting aptitude turned her from the laborious languages to the business course: typing, stenography, and secretarial work, academically easy, but the worst direction for one low in the clerical gift. She wore away her life at work demanding a trait she lacked, ignoring her brilliant inductive reasoning.

Encouraged by test results, an extremely subjective reserved teacher of physical education demonstrated the amazing courage to embrace again a mistakenly renounced preference, and carry it to fruition. At the age of thirty she undertook the advanced study of physiology and eight years later reported that she was assistant professor in one of the country's oldest and largest medical schools with a foundation grant for half-time research. Discomforting reports as a timorous child, and what she regarded an insurmountable want of memory, had forced her to relinquish a youthful ambition for medical research; but when tested she showed every aptitude of the experimental scientist, table XIII, and to her surprise:

| high (grade *A*) | number memory, and |
| low (30th percentile) | accounting aptitude. |

TABLE XIII

APTITUDES OF THE EXPERIMENTAL SCIENTIST

extremely subjective	personality
high	inductive reasoning
high	analytical reasoning
high	tweezer dexterity
high	structural visualization

THIS WOMAN WANTED MEDICAL RESEARCH, BUT WASTED NEARLY TEN YEARS TEACHING PHYSICAL EDUCATION BEFORE APTITUDE TESTS SHOWED HER THAT THE HANDICAP WHICH HAD WORRIED HER THROUGHOUT HER SCHOOLING, AND TURNED HER FROM HER AMBITION, WAS ONLY LOW ACCOUNTING APTITUDE.

By aptitude measurements her only school weakness was grade-C accounting aptitude. This meant low marks, primarily extra hours at homework, but in no way presaged inability for biological research of supreme quality. Subsequently cited by her department head for sound technical ability and shrewd scientific analysis, she still failed an occasional bluebook test even after hours of painstaking preparation; and she returned to the Laboratory at thirty-eight to gain renewed confidence, with the request that it retest her memory, her structural visualization, and her accounting aptitude. She scored convincingly as before, with accounting aptitude low and number memory high, except that in vocabulary she improved beyond the Laboratory's expectations. Originally at the 54th percentile, she now scored at the 93d.

Extremely high accounting aptitude beguiles one into a mistaken path as insidiously as low. Because of his high mark in a HIGH ACCOUNTING APTITUDE paper-and-pencil, mechanical aptitude test, an extremely subjective army private was assigned to aircraft maintenance and, at the end of a depressing year and a half, was discharged because of mental aberrations. In the Human Engineering Laboratory, some months later, he scored low in an apparatus test for structural visualization, but at the 100th percentile in accounting aptitude, a gift which leads to excellence in clerical work, and to an inescapably high score in any aptitude measured by means of paper and pencil. Judging by these results, he belongs in certified public accounting; and eighteen months of enforced mechanical work, in the face of 20th-percentile structural visualization combined with extreme subjectivity, doubtless precipitated his abnormalities. For three and a half years, prior to his army experience, he had been an accountant, working toward his certified public accounting certificate.

An extremely subjective man of twenty-seven, a high-school graduate, married, and soon to be honorably discharged from army service, scored at the 95th percentile in accounting aptitude and low, below the 5th percentile, in structural visualization. When the Laboratory urged that he study accounting, with certified public accounting as his goal, it developed that he had already done so evenings the winter before entering the army; but now hesitated at the required three years' additional preparation, wondering if some sort of production supervision would not suffice as an adequate alternate. Thorough professional training is essential to the lasting happiness of the extremely subjective person. Executive work, with its insistent contacts and strident human problems, gives temporary pleasure but rarely enduring happiness and never a sense of security and permanent accomplishment. Not always does the aptitude pattern of the extremely subjective person indicate a clear profession; but, when it does, the required schooling and training should be obtained despite sacrifices.

In a small mid-western community, the son of the local bank president scored unquestionably high in accounting aptitude, and might start with the initial advantage of his father's financial vocabulary, picked up effortlessly at home. Should extreme subjectivity turn him elsewhere? The mother felt the Laboratory shirked its responsibility by refusing a single rigid recommendation. Although the extremely subjective boy should specialize narrowly, this high-school junior should know various avenues which might use his high accounting aptitude before fixing on one. An extensive statistical and actuarial library might lead to public health, for medicine interested him vaguely, or to a study of population problems. During the great war applied statistics predicted both personnel and material needs. In peace the same technique foretells future sales, plans manufacturing schedules for an even flow to reduce a little the violent peaks and tragic depressions of the past. Through an economics library of his own, which he can well afford, this boy should investigate the theory of banking. With a rare opportunity to follow his father and no doubt become bank president in turn, this extremely subjective boy might gain great happiness from guiding the finances of his community and helping its members with their money struggles; but he might in so doing lose an opportunity to make a lasting contribution toward the stabilization of world economy. For at least three more years he should leave the final decision in abeyance, meanwhile collecting information on which to base a sound final choice.

III

TONAL MEMORY

Low accounting aptitude spoils piano practice, without necessarily showing musical inability. When pressed to play an instrument, to collect phonograph records and a library of scores, an extremely subjective boy rebelled, for piano drill by compulsion had soured everything musical. This boy scores high in tonal memory, high in pitch discrimination, and low in accounting aptitude. No child practices without persuasion; but parents should make certain they drive him toward a pleasurable goal, the two-clef piano, or highly clerical three-clef organ, to challenge one high in accounting aptitude, but the violin or a single-clef woodwind for one who scores low; absence of accounting aptitude diverting the aesthetically gifted child from musical performance as from medicine and law. Extending a relationship found elsewhere, the two staves of piano scripts are four times as laborious to read as one; for in both the clerical and tonal-memory tests errors are proportionate to the square of the number of digits and to the square of the number of notes respectively.

A prominent engineer might easily have drawn his seventeen-year-old son away from his declared interest in music as a life's work, rationalizing that the boy refused to practice the piano and scored at the 40th percentile in structural visuali-

TABLE XIV

APTITUDES USED IN PLAYING A SINGLE-CLEF
MUSICAL INSTRUMENT

extremely subjective	personality
average to high (70th percentile)	pitch discrimination
average to high (65th percentile)	memory for design
average to high (60th percentile)	tonal memory
average to low (40th percentile)	structural visualization
very low (5th percentile)	accounting aptitude

ACCORDING TO APTITUDE SCORES THIS BOY'S CHANCES ARE BETTER IN MUSIC, THE BOY'S INTEREST, THAN IN ENGINEERING, THE FATHER'S PROFESSION.

zation, near enough the 50th percentile decisive line to presume engineering aptitude and enter his father's profession. But with a scientist's viewpoint toward the boy's entire aptitude pattern, table xiv, the father reasoned that, though all aptitude measurements are inaccurate, the boy scores higher in

TABLE XV

UNUSED APTITUDES OF A TAXI DRIVER

extremely subjective   personality
    (zero significant responses on forms AE and FJ)
high (100th percentile)   pitch discrimination
high (95th percentile)   rhythm
high (80th percentile)   abstract visualization
average (70th percentile)   tonal memory
average (70th percentile)   ideaphoria
average (65th percentile)   accounting aptitude
average (40th percentile)   inductive reasoning
average (35th percentile)   English vocabulary
low (21st percentile)   structural visualization

APTITUDES INDICATE THAT THIS MAN SHOULD HAVE FOLLOWED HIS BOYISH AMBITION INTO PROFESSIONAL DANCING; BUT PUBLIC OPINION TURNED HIM AWAY AND AFTER TRYING TO USE HIS IDLE APTITUDES IN STIRRING UP LABOR TROUBLES HE NOW SPENDS TWELVE HOURS A DAY IN DRIVING A TAXI.

three traits, pitch discrimination, memory for design, and tonal memory, than in structural visualization, and in consequence gave the boy every opportunity to acquire musical knowledge.

A long, lean, lanky, straggly-haired youth of thirty-three, with captivating charm, made so vivid a reputation for stirring up labor troubles in a mid-western automobile plant that no industry knowingly adds him to its payroll. He scores as shown in table xv. He wants to compose music and to dance professionally, both perfect expressions of his aptitude pattern; but his father saw no practical future in music, and he now drives a taxi twelve hours a day in Kansas City.

A six-foot boy of fourteen, extremely subjective, with no objective responses on either form AE or FJ of worksample 35, hated the typical boys' camp of the previous summer.

Devoted to his guitar, he belongs somewhere in serious music, or perhaps in professional photography, for he scores as shown in table xvi, and below the 25th percentile in all other aptitudes. Photography uses: pitch discrimination, tonal memory, proportion appraisal, and observation, in about this order. The

TABLE XVI

APTITUDES WHICH SUGGEST PHOTOGRAPHY

100th percentile	in tonal memory
95th percentile	in proportion appraisal
80th percentile	in pitch discrimination
50th percentile	in observation
25th percentile	in accounting aptitude
20th percentile	in ideaphoria
10th percentile	in finger dexterity
10th percentile	in tweezer dexterity
10th percentile	in English vocabulary

THIS BOY LOVES MUSIC WHERE HE COULD USE HIS 100TH-PERCENTILE TONAL MEMORY AND HIGH PITCH DISCRIMINATION. BUT LOW FINGER DEXTERITY IS BOUND TO HANDICAP HIM SOME ON ANY INSTRUMENT; LOW ACCOUNTING APTITUDE WILL ALWAYS SLOW HIS READING FROM SIGHT; AND LOW IDEAPHORIA MAY KEEP HIM FROM TOP PROFESSIONAL BRILLIANCE. HE CANNOT AFFORD TO GAMBLE SOLELY ON MUSIC. HIS APTITUDES SUGGEST PHOTOGRAPHY, BUT HE KNOWS NOTHING ABOUT IT. BECAUSE OF LOW ACCOUNTING APTITUDE AND LOW VOCABULARY HE BELONGS IN A SMALL RECENTLY FOUNDED SCHOOL.

boy should own a camera and organize a photographic laboratory. He loves music; but doubts cloud a gamble on the profession, for finger dexterity and tweezer dexterity, both below the 10th percentile, may limit top performance on almost any instrument, low accounting aptitude handicap the rapid reading of musical scores, low ideaphoria retard brilliance. As a solid base on which to build some unforeseen combination of music and photography the boy needs a rich, full, college background.

Because of low accounting aptitude and low vocabulary he belongs in a small recently founded preparatory school; but he lives an hour and a quarter commuting time from the nearest private school, too large for his low accounting aptitude, and not equipped to teach music at the professional level of his 100th-percentile tonal memory. A distant boarding school might financially jeopardize subsequent education.

Where the right school and the full use of every aptitude are simultaneously unattainable, the latter comes first, for the exercise of a previously idle trait contributes directly to school

TABLE XVII

APTITUDES OF A BORN MUSICIAN

high (89th percentile)	in tonal memory
high (85th percentile)	in pitch discrimination
high (85th percentile)	in finger dexterity
high (85th percentile)	in abstract visualization
extremely subjective (1 significant response)	in personality
low	in ideaphoria
low (20th percentile)	in accounting aptitude
low (16th percentile)	in structural visualization

THIS HIGH-SCHOOL SOPHOMORE LOVES HIS TRUMPET, PLAYS BEAUTIFULLY, BUT WAS CONSIDERING EITHER ENGINEERING OR MEDICINE AS PROFESSIONS WHICH SEEMED TO HIM MORE NORMAL, MORE SOCIALLY ACCEPTABLE THAN MUSIC.

success. With this aim, the boy continued in his local junior high school, though too large, and began going into New York Saturdays for intensive musical training of the highest quality, to use his 100th-percentile tonal memory and 80th-percentile pitch discrimination.

A tall, comely, sedate, high-school sophomore, who loved music passionately, sedulously avoided any mention of the subject throughout his double appointment, for he wanted a normal home environment and looked askance at the exigencies of a musical life, its evening concerts, forced travel. hotel existence, and Bohemian atmosphere. In trying to escape from himself the previous summer, he had gone to camp without his inseparable trumpet, and was miserable. No matter what field he enters, he can never lose music completely.

In aptitudes he scores as shown in table XVII, and below the 25th percentile in all other traits, a pattern which by exclusion leaves concert performing as the only adequate answer.

Low accounting aptitude, at the 20th percentile, may give trouble in the reading of orchestral scores and so handicap conducting; while low ideaphoria means that he should not regard teaching as a primary goal, though an eminent virtuoso may inspire through his own accomplishments, and may even in consequence hold a well-endowed professorial chair. The boy talked of electrical engineering or perhaps medicine, where successful workers average, like himself, extremely subjective in personality. But technical engineers rank high in structural visualization, as opposed to this boy's 15th percentile. With two statistical chances in a hundred, he may survive; but he has done nothing with physics, read nothing on engineering, and the odds seem against it. In the medical world, anatomy and surgery demand structural visualization, but psychiatry is probably non-structural. Here however the boy lacks inductive reasoning, essential to the diagnostician and helpful to the psychiatrist, but far more important he would neglect his musical ability.

No one should be shouldered toward a distasteful life; the Laboratory asks merely that every talented boy know enough to reject a musical career, or any other field, with full understanding of his action and so not regret it later. In this instance the boy scored at the 55th percentile in the vocabulary of music, worksample 295, adequate for his maturity compared with his school associates but not enough to give him an unprejudiced point of view. With average knowledge he thinks in minor terms, for most professional fields call for the sacrifices which this boy thought peculiar to music. The successful engineer may construct a bridge in Brazil, a tunnel in Mexico, a road in Alaska. Ultimately he may establish himself with a permanent home; but so may the great musician. One obvious step was for the boy to build his musical knowledge to perfection, partly so that he might see more clearly musical possibilities, partly because success in every direction including music checks with a large vocabulary.

As low accounting aptitude imposes tiresome hours of clerical drudgery, superior ability in the same trait induces a deceptive facility. An extremely subjective boy, with no objective responses to either form of worksample 35, scored at the

100th percentile in tonal memory, above the 90th percentile in accounting aptitude, and below the 10th percentile in every other characteristic. Only one in a hundred scores as high in tonal memory, with equal chance of possessing the trait; only one in a hundred scores as subjective in worksample 35, with

TABLE XVIII

PROBABLE TRAITS OF THE CONCERT PIANIST

extremely subjective	personality
high	tonal memory
high	finger dexterity
high	tweezer dexterity
high	abstract visualization
high	accounting aptitude
high	rhythm memory
low	structural visualization
high (possibly)	pitch discrimination
high (possibly)	ideaphoria
high (99th percentile)	vocabulary of music
high (99th percentile)	history of music

ONLY ONE PERSON IN ABOUT TEN THOUSAND HAS THIS APTITUDE PATTERN, AND FEWER STILL THE REQUISITE MUSICAL KNOWLEDGE AND WILL TO WORK.

the same certainty of an extremely subjective personality; one in ten thousand showing the pair to a like extent. One in ten scores as high in accounting aptitude, one in ten as low in structural visualization; only one in a million possessing a similar combination of the four; EXALTED MENTAL POWER DISTINGUISHED BY INSTINCTIVE APTITUDE, AND INDEPENDENT OF TUITION, the Century Dictionary definition of GENIUS.

But obscure pitfalls confront this remarkable combination. Completely the pianist in aptitude pattern, table XVIII, he will gain technique easily and believe himself approaching greatness through faultless performance. recognizing too late a meaningless automatism. He lacks ideaphoria, which might supply novelty. His salvation lies in building a sound fund of knowledge to enrich his expression. He naturally chafes at formal schooling which tears him from his piano, and deserves credit for holding his English vocabulary at the mid point. For a nice balance between general background and specialized skill, essential to distinguished achievement, the Laboratory believes in a liberal arts college, carefully picked for size, date of foundation, and excellence in music.

TABLE XIX

Presumed Traits of the Concert Violinist

RATING	WORKSAMPLE	INHERENT APTITUDE
high	215	tonal memory
high	315	pitch discrimination
high	16	finger dexterity
high		abstract visualization
low	4	structural visualization
low	268	accounting aptitude
sometimes		
high	161	ideaphoria

		ACQUIRED KNOWLEDGE
perfect	295	vocabulary of music

THE SINGLE-CLEF VIOLIN SEEMS LESS DEMANDING OF ACCOUNTING APTITUDE THAN THE TWO-CLEF PIANO, TABLE XVIII, AND MORE LIKELY TO TAX PITCH DISCRIMINATION. BOTH USE TONAL MEMORY AND FINGER DEXTERITY.

The parents of a charmingly vivacious, extremely subjective, thirteen-year-old daughter wondered if at the end of the year when she finished eighth grade they should move her from public to private school for greater challenge, for she made consistently high marks with no exertion; also her extremely subjective personality might be lost in the big community high school. She scored as shown in table xx.

Fuller deliberation led to her remaining in public school, carrying her work comfortably with commendable marks because of her high accounting aptitude and grade-B vocabulary, and to her expending the equivalent of private-school tuition in studying music afternoons, Saturdays. and intensively every vacation; for her extremely subjective personality belongs later in one of the professions, or in the fine arts, in painting, writing, or music. Among these, high tonal memory and high accounting aptitude indicate the latter. Harmony and the theory of music would tax her accounting aptitude; piano performance, her tonal memory and tweezer dexterity.

TABLE XX

A MUSICALLY GIFTED EIGHTH-GRADE GIRL

RATING	INHERENT APTITUDE
extremely subjective	personality
high (85th percentile)	accounting aptitude
high	tonal memory
average (grade *B*)	tweezer dexterity
average (grade *B*)	ideaphoria (creative imagination)

	ACQUIRED KNOWLEDGE
average (grade *B*)	English vocabulary

APTITUDE PATTERN OF A CHARMING THIRTEEN-YEAR-OLD GIRL WHO STAYED IN PUBLIC SCHOOL, WHERE SHE WORKED EASILY AND WELL BECAUSE OF HIGH ACCOUNTING APTITUDE AND SATISFACTORY ENGLISH VOCABULARY, AND SPENT THE EQUIVALENT OF PRIVATE-SCHOOL TUITION ON MUSICAL TRAINING OF SUPREME QUALITY, TWO AFTERNOONS EACH WEEK AND SATURDAY MORNINGS.

Four years hence she will meet a similar problem in choosing a college. Facing her future with sympathetic understanding, her parents again favored a small student body, principally because of her unquestioned subjectivity. Staff members at one time favored the intimacy of a small school where everyone speaks and expects cordial recognition in return; but for a thoroughgoing individualist, sufficiently high in clerical ability to turn out rapidly an endless procession of written exercises, the vast impersonal community offers the eclectic privilege of picking friends. Today the Laboratory believes that high or low accounting aptitude outweighs personality in determining school size; and again it urged a large group to tax her accounting aptitude, near a musical center to extend her extra-curricular activities under eminent professional guidance.

Occasionally the staff see clearly a designated direction which parents dismiss as impractical. An extremely subjective boy, who entered his father's restaurant business and ten years later felt that he could stand it no longer, made perfect records in tonal memory and pitch discrimination, but even as a child had done nothing with music. Parents inevitably think of music as leading only to concert performing or to a jazz orchestra. They forget the production of phonograph records, the build-

TABLE XXI

A POTENTIAL VIOLINIST

high (90th percentile)	tonal memory
high (85th percentile)	visual imagination (vision)
high (70th percentile)	observation
low (30th percentile)	structural visualization
low (25th percentile)	accounting aptitude, and
probably objective	
(35th percentile)	personality

THIS TWELVE-YEAR-OLD BOY LOVED THE VIOLIN BUT THE FATHER INSISTED THAT HE STUDY TYPING INSTEAD OF MUSIC.

ing of radio sets and phonographs. The normal, objective father, who wants his son in business, should investigate the great broadcasting corporations, reproduction of voices, of sounds in general, for major executives with these organizations, men who neither sing professionally nor play the piano, except as a hobby, score surprisingly high in tonal memory and pitch discrimination.

Too often one banishes musical aptitudes as aesthetic luxuries, impractical traits developed after retiring from the competitive world, relegating them meanwhile to unproductive radio listening. At mention of music a suburban father countered that he expected his twelve-year-old son to satisfy in pastimes his absorption in art and music, and demanded practical guidance toward a lucrative vocation. This seventh-grade boy scored as shown in table xxi. Prior to the test appointment this solemn father, who fought his own way financially against miserable odds, anticipated enrolling his chubby son in the commercial high school, for typing, stenography, secretarial work, bookkeeping, and accounting, negotiable business tools. But for one who grades D in accounting aptitude the chances of mediocrity or failure are overwhelming. Accounting, law, engineering, and any field, picked by the acceptable sound of the word, are financially impractical unless a boy's chances of rising are better than average, for average incomes in these directions are surprisingly low. This unemotional parent would have preferred an offspring with the clerical speed of the accountant, the structural visualization of the engineer, or the inductive reasoning of the lawyer; but having achieved tonal memory, visual imagination, and observation, it seems to the Laboratory good business to recognize such financial assets; only the playboy with an assured income can afford to expend abilities in hobbies. This only son enjoyed the violin, a perfect single-clef instrument for one high in tonal memory and low in accounting aptitude; but the father's program allowed the boy no spare time for music.

The Laboratory would like the boy to take an academic course, including four years of Latin, in a small preparatory school of fewer than seventy-five pupils, suiting his low accounting aptitude, and then go on to a small, academic, liberal arts college, where he would gain general background. As success depends upon a happy balance between such generalization and more limited specialization, the boy should take violin lessons regularly, perhaps two afternoons a week, with an eminent teacher, for potentially the boy should climb high. He should ideally have his own music room, no matter how tiny, surrounded by well-worn music books, where he can practice at any time of day or night without irritating a tired family. He should study art on Saturday mornings at the local museum. Every summer the Laboratory would like to see him continue his music and art. No one knows the value of protracted summer vacations. Unquestionably a boy needs some out of doors, but if the call of music and art be kept in mind their development often adds to a long summer which might otherwise be partly wasted. Occasional camps offer music and art as integral parts of the summer program; with careful inquiry, excellent teachers of both may often be found near one's own summer home; while boys who spend part of their summers in the city can find classes at the art museum and gifted teachers who are not so busy as in the winter.

In tabular form:

TONAL MEMORY calls for music,

OBSERVATION, for art,

LOW ACCOUNTING APTITUDE demands a small school and either singing or a single-clef instrument,

LOW VOCABULARY means Latin as a basis for more exact building.

TABLE XXII

A COLLEGE GRADUATE IN SEMI-CLERICAL WORK

high (95th percentile)	in tonal memory
high (95th percentile)	in pitch discrimination
high (95th percentile)	in proportion appraisal
high (90th percentile)	in inductive reasoning
high (85th percentile)	in observation
average (45th percentile)	in accounting aptitude
probably objective	in personality
(10 significant responses)	
low (25th percentile)	in structural visualization
low (20th percentile)	in ideaphoria

THIS GIRL BELONGS SOMEWHERE IN THE PHOTOGRAPHIC BRANCH OF THE MOTION-PICTURE INDUSTRY, CLOSELY ASSOCIATED WITH BOTH MUSIC AND ART, WHERE SHE CAN USE TONAL MEMORY, PITCH DISCRIMINATION, AND OBSERVATION, IN PROFESSIONAL PHOTOGRAPHY.

Table xxii shows a college graduate of twenty-three, holding a clerical or semi-clerical job. When asked about music, she responded that she played the violin but not seriously; she rarely practiced, certainly not regularly. Asked about art, which might use the combination of observation and proportion appraisal, she said all her family painted, both her mother and father, an aunt, and an older sister, turning to art in each instance as a pastime, a release from the mundane pressure of earning a living. She looked forward to art, but with no more earnest intent than she granted to music.

By hard purposeful work at her job, she made a place for herself clearly above average, building on no more than a 45th percentile accounting aptitude. With the same energy and consistent purpose based on her outstanding aptitudes she would have gone to the top in some combination of art and music, possibly in some aspect of motion pictures, for tonal memory, pitch discrimination, and observation, belong to both the amateur and professional photographer.

TABLE XXIII

A DISCONTENTED STATISTICIAN

extremely subjective	personality
high (93d percentile)	accounting aptitude
high (90th percentile)	tonal memory
high (90th percentile)	pitch discrimination

THIS UNHAPPY MAN SOUGHT TO USE HIS HIGH ACCOUNTING APTITUDE IN STATISTICS AND HIS EQUALLY HIGH MUSICAL TRAITS IN A HOBBY. THE LABORATORY BELIEVES HE SHOULD HAVE SOUGHT A GOAL COMBINING ALL OF HIS APTITUDES.

With the irresistible passage of irrecoverable youth the happy amalgamation of tonal memory and other aptitudes grows more and more unattainable. An attractive woman of thirty, holding a protected civil service commission with the United States Treasury Department, scored at the 98th percentile in the financial trait, accounting aptitude, low in structural visualization and correspondingly high in the complementary abstract visualization, extremely subjective in personality, and at the 90th percentile in English vocabulary, a perfect syndrome for finance, except that in addition she scored high in the musical gift, tonal memory, high in proportion appraisal, and high in ideaphoria. Capitalizing these stray aptitudes would almost certainly bring fuller happiness, for an English vocabulary at the 90th percentile, coupled with her aptitudes, leads regularly to duties of national scope, with a salary several times her own; but to advocate relinquishing a safe hold for a problematical future in which she might express more aptitudes exceeds the responsibility which any laboratory ought assume.

The statistician shown in table XXIII asked why he should not use his tonal memory and pitch discrimination in some evening musical pastime. While no sign of discontent appeared on the surface, and the man's earnings were above average, he was clearly groping for something, and for a year had been treated by a psychiatrist. To the suggestion that he take music more seriously, he reacted instantly that his working day was of prime importance, a statement which revealed a perpetual internal conflict. Greater satisfaction from music would inter-

TABLE XXIV

Aptitudes which suggest Musical Composing Rather than Performing

extremely subjective	personality
100th percentile	rhythm memory
95th percentile	pitch discrimination
90th percentile	ideaphoria
90th percentile	analytical reasoning
85th percentile	accounting aptitude
85th percentile	tonal memory
55th percentile	abstract visualization
46th percentile	structural visualization
10th percentile	finger dexterity

MOST MEN FIND WORK WHICH USES ONLY ONE OF SEVERAL APTITUDES. THIS MAN USED HIS ACCOUNTING APTITUDE IN ROUTINE CLERICAL WORK, IGNORING HIS TOTAL PATTERN LARGELY BECAUSE AS A YOUNGSTER HIS LOW FINGER DEXTERITY MADE HIM DISLIKE PIANO PRACTICE.

fere with his work. Doggedly holding himself back for fear that he will do too well, he dabbles in music as a pastime, with no adequate accomplishment as recompense. He needs a unified point of view, a goal to use simultaneously, in one direction, his four top traits; though impossible to measure happiness, and study it rigidly, discontent goes regularly with dispersed ability.

After nine years of routine clerical work in a medium sized trust company, a man of 31 scored as shown in table xxiv. Banking used his accounting aptitude, abstract visualization, and low structural visualization, but his ideaphoria led him incessantly astray and his extremely subjective personality kept him year after year at routine work in a minor capacity.

When advised to try musical composing to use his creative imagination, high tonal memory, pitch discrimination, and rhythm, he said that he had played the piano as a child and if he had really belonged in music he felt that he would have gone on at that young age. But he scored at the 10th percentile in finger dexterity and this alone was enough to discourage piano performance. He belongs in composing, not performing.

TABLE XXV

APTITUDE SCORES OF A COLLEGE GRADUATE DISSATISFIED WITH TEACHING COMMERCIAL SUBJECTS IN HIGH SCHOOL

extremely subjective	personality
high (90th percentile)	abstract visualization
high (85th percentile)	accounting aptitude
high (85th percentile)	tonal memory
high (85th percentile)	pitch discrimination
average (65th percentile)	inductive reasoning
low (15th percentile)	ideaphoria
low (11th percentile)	structural visualization

HIGH ACCOUNTING APTITUDE, ABSTRACT VISUALIZATION, AND LOW STRUCTURAL VISUALIZATION, LED THIS MAN TO STUDY TYPING AND STENOGRAPHY. BECAUSE OF EXTREME SUBJECTIVITY HE KNEW THAT HE DID NOT BELONG IN BUSINESS AND TURNED TO TEACHING COMMERCIAL SUBJECTS IN HIGH SCHOOL. HERE HE SUCCEEDED BUT GOT NO SATISFACTION FROM THE WORK. HIS APTITUDES ARE THOSE OF THE CONCERT PIANIST AND MUSIC HAD ALWAYS BEEN HIS ONE ABSORBING HOBBY. HIS EXTREME SUBJECTIVITY SUGGESTS SHIFTING FROM HIGH SCHOOL TO COLLEGE TEACHING AND THEN WORKING GRADUALLY AWAY FROM COMMERCIAL SUBJECTS TOWARD THE TEACHING OF HARMONY AND THE THEORY OF MUSICAL COMPOSITION WHICH WOULD USE ACCOUNTING APTITUDE AS WELL AS HIS MUSICAL TRAITS.

Upon graduating from a small Ohio college, a slight, serious youth, who looked not yet twenty, taught commercial subjects, typing, stenography, and bookkeeping, for two years in a prairie public school, and then came to be tested, asking why his work gave so little joy. He scored as shown in table xxv. About his satisfactory handling of commercial subjects he had no question, applying his accounting aptitude, abstract visualization, and low structural visualization; but he expected a richer reward from work than he finds. He loves classical music, and plays the piano for pleasure. With both the hankering ambition and the native aptitudes to be a concert pianist, there seems at twenty-three little chance of an ample living in this direction. On the other hand, no staid vocation which ignores music offers hope of lasting happiness.

TABLE XXVI

APTITUDES PROBABLY USED IN DRESS DESIGN

	high ideaphoria
	high finger dexterity
	proportion appraisal
	color discrimination
	memory for design
and probably	structural visualization

DRESS DESIGN IS CREATIVE, AND SO USES IDEAPHORIA. THE DRESS DESIGNER USES FINGER DEXTERITY IN HANDLING MATERIALS AND IN MAKING SKETCHES. PROPORTION APPRAISAL, ONCE THOUGHT TO BE GOOD TASTE, IS NOW THOUGHT TO CHARACTERIZE THOSE INTERESTED IN MATERIALS IN CONTRAST TO IDEAS.

The disciplinary problems of high school often harass the extremely subjective teacher, and the Laboratory advised shifting to the higher vocabulary level of college work. Next it suggested changing from bookkeeping to teaching harmony and the theory of musical composition, which would use accounting aptitude as well as his musical traits, and which seemed likely to give him more hours at the piano than high-school teaching, with some hope of advancing toward concert performing if he has the rare ability and the indomitable will.

A housewife, with a daughter away at finishing school and a husband in the army, asked the Laboratory's opinion about an offer to enter dress design, where the ideal pattern includes the aptitudes of table xxvi, and the advisability of continuing music as a hobby. With all but the one most doubtful of the dress designer's traits, this chic housewife, who scores as shown in table xxvii, would undoubtedly enjoy clothing others. But it seems a mistake for any woman to ignore her highest pair of aptitudes, tonal memory and pitch discrimination, both at the 90th percentile. Her incidental mention of music as an enjoyable pastime disclosed her interest.

The staid world hesitates to enter music with little prospect of gaining the top but willingly takes up dress design for a scanty pittance. One who knows nothing of the clothing field dramatizes the freedom, leisure time, and unlimited expression, true only of the financially independent who amuse themselves.

TABLE XXVII

A HOUSEWIFE WHO BELONGS IN MUSIC

extremely subjective	personality
high (90th percentile)	tonal memory
high (90th percentile)	pitch discrimination
high (80th percentile)	abstract visualization
average (70th percentile)	color discrimination
average (68th percentile)	accounting aptitude
average (65th percentile)	proportion appraisal
average (60th percentile)	ideaphoria
average (55th percentile)	memory for design
low (21st percentile)	structural visualization
low (5th percentile)	English vocabulary

THIS WOMAN HAS FOUR TRAITS OF THE DRESS DESIGNER, BUT KNOWS NOTHING OF THE SUBJECT. INSTEAD SHE SHOULD CONTINUE MUSIC, WHICH SHE KNOWS AS A PASTIME, AND WHICH WOULD USE HER TOP THREE TRAITS, SUBJECTIVITY, TONAL MEMORY, AND PITCH DISCRIMINATION.

A living wage from dress design demands exactly as regular and laborious hours as music, and more if one chances to be less well equipped. Dress design for an income is a business rarely enjoyed by extreme subjectivity.

The Laboratory believes it wise to use top aptitudes in a vocation and only lower ones in hobbies. A musically gifted woman, with some corresponding training, has a better chance of ordinary earnings in music than in dress design, of which she knows nothing. Assisting a professional singer, violinist, or other instrumentalist who practices with a piano accompaniment, often gives great pleasure to one high in the musical aptitudes. Playing for a dancing school, or professional dancer, gives a steady income and would keep this woman in the musical world, where she belongs far more than in dress design.

In a Minnesota city a small-delicatessen-store owner decided to sell his stock, together with the good will he had so carefully built, and with the proceeds to study mining engineering, which he heard offered boundless opportunities. But before matriculating he came to be tested. His interests he listed as:

> mining engineering,
> scientific research,
> economics, and
> dramatics.

TABLE XXVIII

An Unsatisfied Delicatessen-Store Owner

extremely subjective	in personality
high (100th percentile)	in proportion appraisal
high (80th percentile)	in tonal memory
average (70th percentile)	in observation
average (70th percentile)	in pitch discrimination
average (65th percentile)	in number memory
average (51st percentile)	in structural visualization
low (15th percentile)	in ideaphoria

THIS MAN SHOULD TAKE MORE SERIOUSLY HIS ACTIVITIES IN THE LOCAL THEATER GROUP, WHERE HE MIGHT FIND OUTLET FOR ALMOST EVERY APTITUDE, TONAL MEMORY AND PITCH DISCRIMINATION IN MUSIC, NUMBER MEMORY IN PREPARING FOR OPENING NIGHT, AND STRUCTURAL VISUALIZATION, IF HE HAS IT, IN SCENE DESIGN AND CONSTRUCTION.

He scored as shown in table XXVIII. As in theory the 51st percentile indicates the full possession of structural visualization, this neighborhood merchant may belong in engineering and research science; but the inaccuracies of the wiggly block and black cube are too great to rely on a score bordering the critical point. With certain proportion appraisal and tonal memory, useless in economics, and the last not used in mining engineering or research, dramatics offers a perfect outlet. Proportion appraisal enters stage design, furniture arrangement, even the placing of characters. Number memory, basic to scheduling, underlies the smooth shift of scenes and complete readiness for opening night. With the same energy, persistence, and thoroughness which he held ready for mining engineering, this man should collect books on the drama, give more time to his local civic theater group, and study stage design and production.

TABLE XXIX

A PROSPEROUS BUT DISSATISFIED SALESMAN

high (100th percentile)	tonal memory
high (90th percentile)	ideaphoria
high (90th percentile)	pitch discrimination
extremely objective	personality
high (80th percentile)	abstract visualization
average (40th percentile)	accounting aptitude
low (30th percentile)	inductive reasoning
low (21st percentile)	structural visualization
average (35th percentile)	English vocabulary

TO THE AGE OF FORTY THIS MAN USED HIS FIVE SALES TRAITS: IDEAPHORIA, OBJECTIVE PERSONALITY, ABSTRACT VISUALIZATION, AVERAGE ACCOUNTING APTITUDE, AND LOW INDUCTIVE REASONING, LUCRATIVELY IN COMMISSION SELLING. THEN HIS IDLE APTITUDES, TONAL MEMORY AND PITCH DISCRIMINATION, SPOILED HIS PEACE OF MIND.

With low ideaphoria and extreme subjectivity he does not belong in selling. On the other hand, he owns a small store and though it gives little pleasure it furnishes a steady and adequate living. As work with the civic theater broadens this man's range of acquaintances and brings him new customers, he should develop an objective, creative assistant.

Partly because minor jobs take no more than one or two traits, partly because groping youth finds the development of one aptitude challenging enough and does not feel the idleness of others, no one starts work using his full strength. But in time unemployed aptitudes turn troublesome. After an energetic life of commission selling, handling in succession copper tubing, oil burning equipment, and machine tools, a heavy man of exactly forty showed the perfect sales pattern, table xxix, but felt dissatisfied. This might be the dawning sense of a low vocabulary, pulling its possessor from a higher level gained through inherent aptitudes; or it might be mere human restlessness, except that it almost never piques the man or woman who uses every aptitude. It seemed more probably due to idle musical traits:

| high (100th percentile) | tonal memory, |
| high (90th percentile) | pitch discrimination, |

used in piano lessons as a child and never touched again. Selling phonograph equipment, quality radios, musical records, sound recording and reproducing devices, or selling photographic equipment, illustrate crude ways of combining sales aptitudes with tonal memory and pitch discrimination.

After establishing herself in a secretarial position at a luxurious salary, a high-accounting-aptitude woman of twenty-eight grew bored with her work. Ten years earlier, in groping for aesthetic expression in art school, and then in writing, she made less progress than she expected; and when tested scored low in creative imagination. In clay modeling, the lack of structural visualization held her back. In the tonal-memory test she made the noteworthy score of one error. Bit by bit it transpired that she gave up the piano when she could not afford to move her own instrument from the Middle West to New York City where she sought her first clerical job. For a while she attended concerts; but they upset her frustrated musical emotions and she stopped. In addition to:

| high | tonal memory, |

she scored with the following traits used in typing:

high	finger dexterity,
high	accounting aptitude,
low	structural visualization,
and extremely subjective	personality,

all aptitudes of the concert pianist. But an executive secretary, who must support herself, can hardly discard an assured salary for the pianoforte. Where then is the practical solution?

As one grows older the voice fades, fingers stumble, and performance becomes increasingly difficult. But knowledge should expand. Yet this girl owned no books. The skeptical world reacts that she could not have been really interested. But she nevertheless made only one error in tonal memory, a conspicuous performance, revealing a poignant trait. Books on music will almost immediately extend her musical knowledge and concurrently her general English vocabulary, demanded for advancement in her own field, for she scores below average.

No one foresees where knowledge leads. No one knows how, within a few years, the world will change. Airplanes, the radio, and now television, create unexpected opportunities. Many who score low in vocabulary claim, and honestly believe, they would acquire the vital knowledge could they but see clearly through the mists of time; and meanwhile someone else, already prepared, grasps the chance. A foothold in these newly expanding fields means advance readiness, sufficient knowledge to set a goal on an ephemeral horizon.

IV

EYEDNESS

In physics, chemistry, astronomy, and mathematics, the older sciences, authorities concur on the fundamentals, but still bicker raucously over up-start theories. In the new field of aptitude testing time's critical influence has not yet set the main course, and honest experimenters will pull in diametrically opposed directions, until extra research, and the gradual discarding of wrong starts, leaves one as probably right. The Laboratory founds conclusions on statistical studies of measured data; but nowhere should its suggestions be followed with greater caution than those based on worksample 236, the test for eye dominance. where authorities wrangle vehemently and no worker can claim omniscience, bewildered parents reporting that another consultant advised their young son to use his right hand and now the Laboratory says left. The author believes that a majority of persons who score unmistakably left eyed in worksample 236 should use the left hand.

An extremely subjective boy, age ten, still in third grade and so two years delayed, scored unmistakably left eyed in this experiment, and wrote with his right hand. In accounting aptitude he scored beneath the normal distribution, implying an extraneous deleterious factor. He read more laboriously than one expects at the bottom of third grade. In speaking he paused perceptibly before voicing each new thought, and then repeated the first syllable several times. He stirred incessantly. The number-checking test he started sitting upright at the table, then drew up a leg, then knelt in his chair, finally discarded the chair and stood, and then dropped his head on his left arm to look slantwise. Such symptoms appear most frequently with boys who score left eyed in worksample 236 and who use primarily the right hand. The Laboratory has not as yet found similar symptoms with any boy who scores equally left eyed and who uses his left hand.

This brings up instantly the advisability of the left-eyed boy shifting to the use of his left hand, for many factors indicate the hand should be shifted; the eye, as indicated by worksample 236, revealing inherent sidedness. By social custom every sophisticated person shakes hands with the right, and no one with the left. Leaving this artificially prescribed ritual, six per cent write with the left hand, a highly trained activity but one in which schools try to allow some freedom of choice, though the use of one hand in preference to the other is probably conditioned from the moment the parent first holds the child's hand in the cradle. Going from highly cultivated writing, to progressively less rigidly trained activities, through tennis, kicking a football, to throwing a stone, one finds the left handers increasing gradually to eleven per cent. But even the casual toss of a stone is influenced by the child's imitation of others. The dominant eye is the option which seems least influenced by environment, and here twenty-five per cent choose the left. Because the eye seems less influenced by training than the hand, and so a more reliable indication of inherent sidedness, the Laboratory believes in cultivating the hand to imitate the eye, where serious outward complications accompany crossed dominance, even at the risk of exacerbated transitory trouble, for the transition from the traditional right to the odd left temporarily exaggerates symptoms which the shift ultimately lessens, and should be undertaken only at one's own discretion, with determination to persist slowly through the initial disturbing stage.

A delightful, right-handed college girl, a member of the Laboratory staff, wholly free of the symptoms which ordinarily accompany crossed dominance, scored left eyed in worksample 236; and determined upon changing to her own left hand, believing that otherwise she could not well advise examinees. Within a few weeks she developed a frightening and foreign tenseness. In her enthusiasm and confidence she undoubtedly went too fast; but even with patience the effects of converting from one hand to the other are deep-seated and startling. The author himself would shift to the hand which coincides with the eye, in the belief that otherwise a mental strain renders one unduly sensitive to nervous ailments.

At least two conditions ordinarily unite for the beginning of a physical and mental illness. First, in the case of a contagious disease, a low resistance, a readiness for acceptance; and, second, actual contact. Since anyone who travels in trains or subways, enters a city, or even drinks a glass of water, may meet an unwelcome noxious germ, a gradually strengthened resistance is always a wise precaution. In the case of nervous and mental diseases, including perhaps the most dreaded polio or infantile paralysis, there must probably be first a predisposition and second the stress of adverse circumstances which brings on the attack. An eminent alienist once said: Everyone has the predisposition; and certainly everyone encounters difficulties somewhere on life's tumultuous course. Again one solution is to build up an inherent mental vitality, partly by removing internal frictions which tap nerve strength. A strong man may succeed for years at work which conflicts with his aptitude pattern; and then go suddenly to pieces at some inimical combination of distresses. With two extremely subjective salesmen who ultimately broke down nervously, the cause may not have been subjectivity in sales, but this seems to the Laboratory a contributing element. In like manner the forced use of the right hand, by a naturally left-eyed and so left-sided person, does not cause emotional, glandular, and nerve diseases, but may sap nerve strength to a point where they take root.

Battered by ten years as sales clerk and floorwalker in an uncle's department store where extreme subjectivity, no significant response on form AE, rendered him miserably out of place. a bewildered man of twenty-eight resorted, in sheer desperation, to mechanical work with his father-in-law, who owned and operated a pencil factory. But the son scores low in structural visualization, and by nature belongs in an intellectual profession, an obvious absurdity with an English vocabulary below the 5th percentile. This worried man stammered badly and scored predominantly left eyed. Believing his speech block remediable, the Laboratory recommended that he tentatively cultivate his left hand. Convinced by his own performance of worksample 18, the tweezer-dexterity test, where he scored faster with his left than with his habitual right, he began carrying his handkerchief in his left-hand trouser pocket, lighted cigarettes with his left hand, and once a day signed his name with his untutored left.

The Laboratory could probably have sensed his left eyedness at age six with a fair chance of lessening the speech impediment at a time when two or three years' training is not so laborious as twenty years later. It could also have measured a low vocabulary as early as age seven, perhaps at age six, with justified hope of raising it materially. At twenty-eight its building is tedious; but the man must start or spend the rest of his life in uncongenial surroundings. For encouragement he should return at the end of a year for a second test appointment and further stimulation, although he can hope for little apparent gain for double that period. He bought the Vocabulary Builder and a complete set of brochures, to gain a clearer picture of himself; meanwhile he should continue factory work, a long, slow, remedial program for any man so badly misplaced, one particularly difficult to present in low-vocabulary terms, but the only one which the Laboratory believes holds hope of ultimate adjustment.

By the age of 38 an internationally cultured woman had scored three brilliant feats. As principal assistant to a leading theatrical promoter, she had been largely responsible for the sparkling originality of his dramatic settings. Then she gained a free hand as head of stage design and play production in a huge state university. This she left for an exciting part in the colorful design and subsequent operation of a memorable world's fair. Then she married. Years later, with two children of her own, this vital personality grew impatient to regrasp her active creative life, and she assumed the training of grammar-

TABLE XXX

GREAT DESIGNER OF COLOR EFFECTS

extremely subjective	in personality
high (95th percentile)	in tweezer dexterity
high (90th percentile)	in ideaphoria
high (90th percentile)	in finger dexterity
average (70th percentile)	in pitch discrimination
low (50th percentile)	in structural visualization
low (15th percentile)	in tonal memory
low (10th percentile)	in analytical reasoning
low (5th percentile)	in inductive reasoning
low (5th percentile)	in proportion appraisal
left	in eyedness
right	in handedness
average (65th percentile)	in English vocabulary

THIS ARTISTIC WOMAN USED IDEAPHORIA IN GAINING AN INTERNATIONAL REPU-
TATION FOR SPECTACULAR COLOR EFFECTS, FINGER DEXTERITY IN THE SELECTION
OF FINE FABRICS, AND PITCH DISCRIMINATION IN A GENERAL NICENESS OF SENSE
PERCEPTION. CROSS DOMINANCE, LEFT EYEDNESS WITH RIGHT HANDEDNESS,
CAUSED A NERVOUS TENSION WHICH MAY HAVE CONTRIBUTED TO HER SUCCESS,
BUT WHICH ALSO INTERFERES WITH HER OWN PERSONAL SATISFACTION.

school and high-school classes in play production. After two years she came to the Laboratory, unhappy in teaching, disliking the inevitable disciplinary problems, craving an aesthetic polish beyond school pupils, and ready to abandon the theatrical world for a new exploit. She scored as shown in table xxx.

With this aptitude pattern the Laboratory could indicate creative work, because of unmistakable ideaphoria, in a professional and artistic atmosphere because of extreme subjectivity, and might suggest the handling of fine textures, because of finger dexterity. Her extremely subjective yearning for perfection found more gratification at the college level, where she had once succeeded and been happy, than in teaching children; also there are fewer disciplinary problems. But she had a rare opportunity in much needed creative work with children, under a sympathetic and inspiring headmaster, if she could meet the extrinsic obstacles. In behavior she was tense, emotional, high strung. This may have sprung from her job dissatisfaction, but seemed to the test administrator to come in part from the dominant use of her right hand with a score of left eyedness in worksample 236. She might relax her dangerous tenseness by learning new manual operations with the left hand and ultimately relearning standard tasks.

Sometimes a test appointment consists in eliminating nonessentials, looking for the single factor which contributes to an understanding. Contemplating a vocational change, a New England stenography teacher hoped for more salary as confidential secretary to an industrial executive, but scored at the 10th percentile in accounting aptitude. Cramped in vocational education he asked about a factory job. Again his aptitudes said no, for he scored low in structural visualization and equally low in both finger and tweezer dexterity. Low observation left him but slim chance of rising through the inspection department.

This teacher appeared well adjusted, quiet, and relaxed, with no signs of fretful restlessness; but he scored left eyed in worksample 236 and right handed. As the test administrator described the outward conflicts which frequently accompany crossed dominance, the man listened absorbed, asked questions, and at length revealed his real worry. Periodically for years he stayed away from work, sometimes several weeks at a time, from nervous exhaustion. The left-eyed finding gave him exactly what he wanted, a vital pivot about which he might turn for greater satisfaction and worldly comfort.

But the test administrator had not finished; for the man scored at the 35th percentile in English vocabulary and should build this acquirable asset. Together with the leisurely cultivation of his left hand this gave him a nucleus for his errant thoughts and a constructive direction for a full year's program. He promised to return in twelve months, for a check on his vocabulary, for a more extensive knowledge inventory, and for additional aptitude tests with a consequent filling out of his inherent pattern, for the six hours of a double appointment allow the measurement of no more than ten or twelve aptitudes out of some eighteen now recognizable and a possible hundred still unknown. In two three-hour sessions, no

TABLE XXXI

A TRAIN DISPATCHER
AFTER TWENTY-ONE YEARS' SERVICE

extremely subjective	in personality
at the 100th percentile	in tweezer dexterity
above the 90th percentile	in proportion appraisal
high	in memory for design
high	in tonal memory
average	in accounting aptitude
low	in number memory
low	in structural visualization

THIS MAN BELONGED ORIGINALLY SOMEWHERE IN THE FINE ARTS. ROUTING AND DISPATCHING OF ALL TYPES USES NUMBER MEMORY WHICH HE LACKS.

one can claim to remake a man's life; but, to an examinee who thinks of the initial appointment as the first of a series, the Human Engineering Laboratory offers enough to fill the year which intervenes before the next.

A long, lean, train dispatcher with twenty-one years' service said that he had never enjoyed his railroad job. In addition to the aptitudes of table xxxi, he scored at the 51st percentile for his age in English vocabulary, and unmistakably left eyed but used his right hand. Scheduling, routing of all kinds, demands number memory, where he scored low. Without the symptoms: stuttering, restless moving about, reading difficulties, he came with a profound desire to get more from life. The training of his left hand might remove an elusive internal friction. Because of his expressed dissatisfaction with life, but with less assurance than if he stuttered noticeably or showed abnormal nervousness, the author believes he should experiment with some simple left-hand activity, so slowly and gradually that its full cultivation might fill a calendar year.

This man also scores at the 100th percentile in tweezer dexterity. Normally every aptitude should be used as a part of a man's job. In this case the incorporation of tweezer dexterity seemed impossible and he should probably find a hobby, although rarely a real solution.

A grievously worried widow, supporting herself, brought her extremely subjective eighth-grade son to be tested for right or left sidedness, which she hoped might throw light on his speech block, for his vocal cords went through the contractions of utterance with no sound and, when he suddenly spoke, he repeated the audible phrase several times. In consequence he often sat silent from anticipated embarrassment. The father had been left handed; and the mother justly felt that the boy, who used his right, should perhaps change. But he scored unmistakably right eyed in worksample 236 and in the opinion of the writer should continue with his right hand. In imitation of his father, he may use his left hand consciously more than appears in the test, but no more than he should.

For a possible lessening of his speech impediment one must turn elsewhere and remove sources of emotional frustration. This boy had no basement workshop, had never tapped his high structural visualization; and when this trait lies idle it simulates unused left handedness. The mother, a long-laboring seamstress, depended on public education where physics and chemistry come in the junior and senior years of high school, still three years off. Languages, which play so large a part in early education, demand low structural visualization, not high. The boy should have good tools, a simple work bench, clay for modeling, outlets for structural visualization, a trait less apt than others to have natural expression in modern urban life. As further hindrances, the boy scored low in both accounting aptitude and English vocabulary. He belongs in a small school, financially out of the question. By himself he must acquire techniques for mollifying, if not overcoming, his low accounting aptitude, and build his vocabulary to be more confident of the words he wants.

Test administrators inadvertently apply the term CROSS DOMINANT to one who scores left eyed and who uses predominantly the right hand. This gives the erroneous impression that eye dominance, measured in any way, is the essential factor; and also leaves opportunity for the common question of how much visual acuity affects dominance. An oculist writes that in one case his determination of eye dominance disagrees with the Laboratory's record. Here vocabulary misleads. Actually the Laboratory knows little of dominance as a whole. The foregoing recommendations apply to one who scores left eyed in worksample 236, regardless of cause. Not everyone at the left end of the scoring scale, who uses the right hand, shows the frequent symptoms of nervousness, laborious reading, and speech blocks, and these exceptions may score left eyed because of acuity differences, or for some other extraneous reason; but the Laboratory's recommendations depend upon test scores only, not upon eye dominance unless measured by worksample 236. It seems desirable therefore to find or invent a term, independent of all implications. The following extract comes from a letter by James Ricks, for four years a member of the Laboratory staff:

'I can discover no words or roots with the meaning LEFT available for use in English which have not at one time and another carried also the meaning unlucky, ill omened, bad, or pernicious. It is interesting to note, however, that while the words *sinister*, *laevus*, and *scaevus*, were being used in this sense by the Romans, they had exactly the opposite sense when referring to augurs. This is because the good signs were supposed to appear in the east, the bad ones in the west, and the Romans, in looking for signs, faced south which placed the east on their left hand; hence LEFT in this connection meant fortunate, lucky, propitious. The Greeks, on the other hand, faced north when auguring, and for them the left was the bad side under all circumstances.

'While the word SINISTER has continued in English with its evil connotations, the words *laevus* and *scaevus*, together with their associated noun and adverb forms, have not. I can discover no words now in use based on *scaevus*, but it does not seem suitable for our purposes because of its unfortunate orthographical and phonetic resemblance to SCAVENGER, SCURVY, and SCABROUS. An abnormally high percentage of words beginning SCA- or SCAV- have unpleasant connotations.

' The word *laevus*, however, does turn up nowadays in some scientific terms; an example from the field of physical chemistry being LAEVOGYRATE or LEVOGYRATE, referring to substances which rotate polarized light to the left. And so far as I can discover, no word now in use which has *laevus* as its root has any pleasant or unpleasant connotations *per se*.

' Both *laevus* and *scaevus* come originally from Greek roots: λαιός (*laios*) and σκαιός (*scaios*) respectively. But the Greek in this case does not offer so good possibilities as the Latin for forming combined words which might stand for left handedness or left sidedness. There is another Greek word, ἀριστερός (*aristeros*), which seems to mean left, but I have not been able to check it thoroughly enough to be confident of our right to use it legitimately in the way you want to; there are apparently disagreements as to the propriety of its use in certain senses by various classes of Greeks, and I gather that somehow it may not really have meant left at all.

' To return to the purpose of this letter, it seems to me that while there is no really perfect candidate for the honor of being made into a new word for left sidedness, *laevus*, anglicized into the prefix LAEVO- or LEVO-, has many advantages.

' Picking a good suffix is even tougher, or at least seems so to me. Possibilities I have considered include:

LEVODOMINANCE	LEVODOMINATE,
LEVOLATERALITY	LEVOLATERAL or LAEVOLATE,
LEVOVERSION	LEVOVERT,
LEVOMANUALITY	LEVOMANUAL,

the first word designating the condition or quality, and the second the person. I do not really like either the looks or the sound of any of them. MANUAL, of course, is too purely a word signifying hand; while -VERSION or -VERT implies a turning toward the use of one side or the other, and should properly be used, I think, to characterize a BEHAVIOR rather than an inherent, fundamental trait; just as EXTRAVERSION and INTROVERSION describe modes of behavior, action, or thinking, which may be consciously modified, and are not synonymous with what we conceive to be OBJECTIVE or SUBJECTIVE personality. Also from Stedman's Medical Dictionary there already are such words as LEVOVERSION and LEVOVERT in the English language, defined as: turning toward the left, and applied in medical parlance to such things as an eyeball or a foot.

'LATERAL really is misused in a word like this since it applies properly rather to a direction than to a place where a motion occurs; it sounds more like a hand moving toward the left than it does like a left hand or a tendency to use the organs on the left side more frequently. LATERAL also connotes, I think, a distinction of sides with reference to a horizontal rather than a vertical, though this point may be unimportant. Finally, the difficulty with -DOMINANCE or -DOMINATE is that these suffixes rob the prefix LEVO- of its rightful place of dominance in the word; i.e. the word LEVODOMINANCE seems to imply a word LEVOSUBMISSION or LEVOSUBMISSIVE as its opposite or complement, instead of standing naturally opposed to DEXTRODOMINANCE.

'LEVOCOSTAL was a possibility suggested by a friend of mine, but it unfortunately runs afoul of the fact that the suffix -COSTAL, from the Latin costa, a rib, refers to side only in the sense of a physical side, like the side of a box or the side wall of a body, or in the original sense of a rib.

'Such are the facts of the matter so far as I have been able to run them down. I hope they will suffice to enable you to make a decision. For my own opinion, I should say that I personally much prefer the plain, simple, straightforward term LEFT SIDEDNESS to any of these artificial terms. Granted it is not a particularly lovely word, and would not go so well in a poem, it has for the purposes of scientific exposition, of good factual writing, the enormous advantages of being clearly understood and unpretentious. Of the various compounds suggested I think I might possibly utter faint praise for LEVODOMINANCE and LEVODOMINATE, and practically no praise for any of the others.'

Despite James Ricks' liking for the straightforward term LEFT SIDEDNESS, it gives perpetual trouble from those who, because of its simplicity, believe they can determine SIDEDNESS in any way and then apply the Laboratory's recommendations to the result, forgetting their dependence solely upon scores in worksample 236. Chemistry has found it a great convenience to have unmistakable terms for its chemical elements, and similar advantages should hold for separate aptitudes. After further consideration the Laboratory has settled on: LEVOLATE and DEXTROLATE.

v

READING DIFFICULTIES

Slow reading, which may accompany low accounting aptitude, need not delay normal mental development if a child be given knowledge by other channels. An extremely subjective girl, tested first in seventh grade at age twelve, scored at the 14th percentile when she read the English vocabulary test silently to herself, the ordinary practice with adults; but at the 48th percentile in a second form given orally, the examiner reading aloud the phrase, including the test word, then the test word alone to emphasize it, and then each choice, pointing simultaneously. Three years later, as a high-school sophomore, the same girl scored at the 52nd percentile, taking the test in the usual manner, having learned to read in the meantime. Reading the test aloud at age twelve gave probably the accurate indication of her genuine word knowledge; for a vocabulary improvement in three years from the 48th to the 52nd percentile is reasonable, an improvement from the 14th to the 52nd far less likely. With the child who gains a large thinking and speaking vocabulary early in life, through environment, reading aloud, and general conversation, reading vocabulary ultimately attains the same level. For this reason parents, brothers, sisters, and friends, should read aloud to all children who enjoy it and who show any trace of reading blocks. Otherwise vocabulary lags in the early years and never later builds rapidly enough to reach the top. Measured findings do not substantiate the fear of both parents and teachers that reading aloud retards a child's own skill.

Low. 5th percentile. accounting aptitude, shambling awkwardness due in part to the graceless antagonism of right-hand usage with a dominant left eye, LEVOLATE, and in part to a medical history of early infantile paralysis, together with extreme subjectivity, all combined to envelop another fifteen-year-old child in an aura of dull feeblemindedness. She entered crying because she had to take tests, and read so laboriously that she could not do worksample 176, the easiest vocabulary. But when the same test, and later a more difficult one, were read aloud, she scored at the 80th percentile. Grasping this unexpected lead, the test administrator began treating her as a normal grown-up, to which she responded delightfully. In regard to sidedness, she enjoyed drawing with her left hand, and volunteered to use it more. Although limited financially, her parents granted her a small allowance to haunt second-hand book stores and to build a personal library. This gave a sense of possession and intimacy. Thereafter, when she heard a book discussed, instead of feeling shut off from the whole literary world by her ungainliness and laborious reading, she knew the book's place on her own shelves and sensed its physical ownership. In addition her mother and father began reading aloud evenings and Sundays, books which they enjoyed, a practice over which they had previously hesitated for fear it would retard her own reading.

VI

ABSTRACT VISUALIZATION

Unmistakably low scores in the wiggly blocks, worksamples 3 and 4, in the formboards, worksample 230, in the black cube, worksample 246, or in the recent piped cube, worksample 300, indicate a lack of structural visualization, and simultaneously the positive presence of a component, which the Laboratory tentatively calls ABSTRACT VISUALIZATION. Two decades ago, before any thought of twinned traits, the uniformly low structural scores obtained by accountants suggested not only lack of this mechanic's trait but a direct contribution by its counterpart. Later, lawyers scored similarly low, and still later bankers. Finally the bimodal curve materialized for personality, indicating two distinct types of people with a gap between, direct evidence of opposing traits.

Popular science accepts blue eyes and brown as a natural pair, and rigid geneticists concede the dichotomy of inherited physical factors; but it took twenty years of gradually deepening research to evolve a like concept of compensating aptitudes. Architects, engineers, and research scientists, diemakers, toolmakers, sculptors, and surgeons, all score high in structural visualization; all deal with material, three-dimensional objects, and in consequence the trait common to these workers has been termed STRUCTURAL VISUALIZATION. Salesmen, accountants, musicians, lawyers, writers, and bankers, dealing with abstract intellectual concepts, score as consistently low in structural visualization, and their common trait has been called, with less certainty, ABSTRACT VISUALIZATION.

By means of his structural visualization a low-vocabulary mechanic earns a comfortable living; then, as he adds to his acquired knowledge, he rises to machinist; and perhaps later, still higher in the vocabulary scale, to draftsman, engineer, or research scientist. But the allelomorphic aptitude, abstract visualization, is of no avail without exact words to embody its rarefied concepts. Abstract visualization together with the independent aptitude, extreme subjectivity, demand three or four college years, even ideally a graduate degree, and with no academic training, and without the precise English words which ought to follow, lead often to abject failure.

A maddening predicament for the test administrator is the low-vocabulary boy or girl who insists upon being told exactly what to do. Unquestionably the extremely subjective person should aim toward a specific goal; but equally surely a low vocabulary precludes such a goal. An extremely subjective boy, table XXXII, took a year and a half of college engineering, joined the army, was later honorably discharged, and then came to see if he should return to his engineering course. When the test administrator advised a transfer, because of low structural visualization, to the academic course in the same college, the boy insisted that he disliked English, history, Latin, and foreign languages generally, and enjoyed mathematics, because of his 70th percentile accounting aptitude. To use this last trait in a non-structural field the administrator suggested an exploratory course in statistics, in economics, or in accounting. But the boy expressed indifference, and these would probably not use his high creative imagination. Until this boy raises his English vocabulary it will be impossible to convey in words the intangible goal he should seek. There is writing, historical research, the study and classification of

TABLE XXXII

AFTER A YEAR AND A HALF
OF COLLEGE ENGINEERING

high (90th percentile)	in ideaphoria
high	in abstract visualization
high	in tonal memory
high	in memory for design
average (70th percentile)	in accounting aptitude
low	in structural visualization
very low (5th percentile)	in English vocabulary

BECAUSE OF THIS BOY'S ABSTRACT VISUALIZATION, THE LABORATORY BELIEVES ACADEMIC TRAINING WOULD BE OF MORE VALUE THAN CONTINUING ENGINEERING, BUT COULD OFFER NO SPECIFIC RECOMMENDATION WHICH APPEALED.

nature: insects, flowers, birds, snakes. "But I am not interested", declares the extremely subjective person; and for exactly this reason the Laboratory finds it nearly impossible to make positive suggestions, for there are some ten thousand extremely subjective, non-structural activities, and the chance is slim, especially with the low-vocabulary person who has little general knowledge, of stumbling on that particular one which might interest him if he had sufficient knowledge to grasp its allure.

A forceful, ambitious mother wanted her twelve-year-old scion to prepare for surgery. Like the surgeon he scored extremely subjective in personality, but low in structural visualization. To the anticipated query: how precisely can a boy use abstract visualization, indicated by a low structural score, combined with a 90th-percentile ideaphoria, the Laboratory mentioned creative writing. The mother countered that the boy always got low school marks in English composition and could not write. For medicine, she acknowledged the need of college training, of medical school and internship, of surgical knowledge and operating room skills, conceding that at his childish age he could neither practice medicine nor operate successfully; but she evaded blindly parallel training as indispensable to professional writing. The verbal tools, lacked by this low-vocabulary boy, can be acquired, but not the structural visualization of the surgeon. The writer's aptitudes are as rare as the surgeon's and, supplemented by as thorough training, lead to as great success.

Talbot Hamlin proposes that abstract visualization is an intellectual insight into human actions, differentiating this from the independent pair of aptitudes, grouped under the heading PERSONALITY, and often wrongly described in much the same words. The extremely subjective person demands individual freedom; objectivity by contrast is not so much an understanding of people as an easy, day-to-day enjoyment of humanity *en masse*, a feeling with other human beings. Abstract visualization then becomes a rational comprehension of their emotions. Salesmen score objective in personality, relishing their fellows, and high in abstract visualization, revealing, on Mr. Hamlin's hypothesis, an understanding of mankind essential to successful selling. Writers score equally high in abstract visualization and follow human thoughts in consequence; but unlike salesmen they score extremely subjective in personality and so enjoy or at least do not rebel at the long, lone hours required to reduce this understanding to words. Lawyers comprehend reactions, abstract visualization, and at the same time spend hours seeking ancient precedents, preparing briefs, and complying with legal formalities, and so like writers score extremely subjective in personality. Technical scientists, high in structural visualization, certainly demonstrate an appalling blindness to personal sensitivities, but work happily alone, extreme subjectivity.

A non-structural boy, who scores objective in personality and who studies engineering by mistake, turns such technical knowledge to advantage in manufacturing executive work. An extremely subjective boy cannot afford a similar misstep; he should avoid failure, and waste no time on subjects unrelated to the field he must ultimately embrace intimately.

Every boy who scores HIGH in structural visualization, between the 71st and 100th percentiles, should use the trait; another who scores LOW, at the 30th percentile or below, should with equal consciousness use abstract visualization, pointing toward the manipulation of detached ideas. One who scores AVERAGE, in the doubtful mid region from the 31st percentile to the 70th, possesses structural visualization or its opposite, abstract visualization, but not both. For men and boys of all ages, the presumed division occurs between the 50th and 51st percentiles. A boy rated AVERAGE, who scores between the 31st and 50th percentiles, should theoretically use abstract visualization and avoid tangible structures. Another between the 51st and 70th percentiles, also ranked AVERAGE, should enter a structural field.

With women of all ages the corresponding critical line falls at the 75th percentile; for only a quarter of women inherit this mechanic's trait compared with half of men. In practice most women who score HIGH, from the 71st to the 100th percentile, should seek some sort of structural outlet, while those who score average or low should avoid structural occupations and professions.

An extremely subjective girl scored high enough in three trials of the wiggly block to presume the trait, but low in the fourth, averaging at the 55th percentile, well below the critical 75th for women. In the black cube she scored twice at the 50th percentile, coinciding with the average of her four wiggly-block trials. Although nearing the end of her high-school junior year she had taken no chemistry, no physics or biology, and had met trouble with plane geometry, a semi-structural subject. On the other hand, her declared interest in medicine seemed too keen to ignore. If turned away by low structural visualization she might easily regret the decision for life. In numerous such instances distressed parents force an immediate, irrevocable, and often wrong judgment. With every aptitude of the writer, as listed in table XXXIII, this girl herself suggested that she might write about medicine, a perfect solution, for her ambition was more a desire to help humanity than a love of science. Aptitude scores, presented as factual findings, enable such a girl to evolve her own point of view; and parents should restrain their insistence on concrete recommendations in a digested report.

The undeniable success in medicine of two low-structural persons, one a man, the other a woman, both extremely sub-

TABLE XXXIII

TRAITS OF THE WRITER

high	ideaphoria
high	inductive reasoning
high	analytical reasoning
high	abstract visualization
low	structural visualization
extremely subjective	personality

THIS TABLE LISTS APTITUDES WHICH THE LABORATORY BELIEVES ARE LIKELY TO FIND OUTLET IN WRITING.

jective in personality, does not mean that all low-structural people should follow in their steps. Aptitude testing turns the ordinary youth, with no steadfast ambition, away from fields where his chances are slight; and apprises another, with a fixed goal, of potential hurdles before he encounters them as unexpected shocks. Urged irresistibly toward medicine from early childhood, both of these low-structural medical students failed first-year anatomy and would have dropped medicine at that point had the Laboratory not previously warned them of just this eventuality. Both attribute their perseverance at least in part to aptitude tests, for medical school might have dropped them except for prescience of structural failures and the stated non-structural aspirations of each.

An extremely subjective boy, age 15, attracted both by experimental chemistry and by his concept of a physician's life, scored as shown in table xxxiv. Low accounting aptitude indicates a small school, with a total enrollment not above seventy-five pupils, low English vocabulary one recently founded, as discussed more fully in APTITUDES AND THE LANGUAGES. Extreme subjectivity means a profession; but not law because of low inductive reasoning. With tonal memory as his top trait the boy should do something with music; but not with the two-clef piano which he tried and disliked because of his low accounting aptitude. Outside of school he should build his vocabulary, following the formulated laws of learning, and using the Laboratory's VOCABULARY BUILDER.

TABLE XXXIV

A 15-YEAR-OLD BOY TRYING TO DECIDE BETWEEN
RESEARCH CHEMISTRY AND MEDICINE

average (60th percentile)	tonal memory
average (50th percentile)	structural visualization
average (40th percentile)	pitch discrimination
average (40th percentile)	ideaphoria
low (30th percentile)	accounting aptitude
low (20th percentile)	English vocabulary
low (10th percentile)	inductive reasoning
extremely subjective	personality

APTITUDE TESTS DID NOT HELP THIS BOY IN MAKING THE CHOICE HE BROUGHT TO THE LABORATORY. BUT HIS LOW ACCOUNTING APTITUDE INDICATES A SMALL SCHOOL; HIS LOW ENGLISH VOCABULARY, ONE RECENTLY FOUNDED. BOTH OF HIS AMBITIONS DEMAND MORE EXACT KNOWLEDGE THAN HE POSSESSES.

So much seems clear, but does not settle the employment question of chemistry versus medicine, with which the boy came to be tested. The sciences use structural visualization, often an indispensable asset. Were the test invariably accurate a boy at the 50th percentile lacks the artisan's trait, and should use instead abstract visualization in the manipulation of ideas; while another at the 51st percentile should enter a structural field with confidence in his full possession of the trait. But the recognized errors of the test are such that any score within ten or fifteen percentiles of the decisive center gives no certain indication. The boy's aptitude pattern shows numerous assured negatives; business, sales, advertising, and politics, are objective, while he scores extremely subjective; law and teaching use high inductive reasoning; while accounting itself demands high accounting aptitude. He should continue chemistry and pre-medical work, which remain as two open avenues. But whatever his occupational future the boy belongs in a small preparatory school, and later in a small liberal arts college. He must build his English vocabulary, for any profession suitable to extreme subjectivity demands sound knowledge. The boy should be further tested annually to plot his vocabulary development from year to year.

VII

HIGH IDEAPHORIA

A non-conforming boy of eleven dissipated precious hours in rambling visions, with no conception of life's realities. When called on in class, he was off roaming some dream countryside. At one stage he pictured himself an aeronautical engineer and talked so convincingly of airplanes with flapping wings that his father bought woodworking tools and a carpenter's bench, which the day-dreamer never touched. Considering themselves unfit to cope with so maddening a child, his parents decided on military school, but brought him first to be tested, table xxxv.

Turning brilliant imagination, shown by a high score in ideaphoria, to constructive use means taking advantage of every known principle. His low accounting aptitude calls for a small school. In his present class of thirty he recites so seldom that his roving mind strays between whiles; in a class of four or five his verbal imagination would lead the group.

The mother offered the typical resistance. The boy would live in the tumultuous world ultimately and should accustom himself to the bustling school. The Laboratory believes the exact reverse; education should furnish fertile soil for the rich cultivation of incipient aptitudes and the harvesting of bountiful knowledge. A physical director trains a growing boy to lift a slight weight in preparation for the heavier one, to run a short distance in training for the mile, to ski a gentle slope before the jump; but parents throw a low-accounting-aptitude boy into a thousand-pupil school, counting on this drastic treatment to teach him cooperation; like lifting too big a load, it frequently strains him beyond recovery.

To build basic word knowledge, called for by the combination of ideaphoria and extreme subjectivity, each boy must start at his own low-vocabulary level. But the locality where this boy lived offered no suitable private school, small and recently founded, such as he needs; and, like many others, the

TABLE XXXV

An Eleven-Year-Old Day-Dreamer

extremely subjective	personality
high	ideaphoria
low	accounting aptitude
low	structural visualization

THIS BOY BELONGS IN A VERY SMALL SCHOOL WHERE HIS VIVID IMAGINATION, IDEAPHORIA, HAS FREE OUTLET IN CLASSROOM DISCUSSIONS, UNHAMPERED BY HIS LOW ACCOUNTING APTITUDE, WHICH MAKES ALL WRITING LABORIOUS.

mother objected to sending her child away, although she came with military school in mind. The Laboratory advances no claim to balance such facts and principles; worried parents must reach their own decisions; but the selection of the right school and college warrants judicial consideration.

Although ideaphoria is the top trait of teachers, when too high and combined with extreme subjectivity it leads to a feeling of frustration which not only stops actual progress but may lead to a nervous breakdown. A fourth-grade teacher came with a feeling of inferiority which had twice driven her to seek psychiatric help. Every afternoon by three-thirty, when school closed, she was exhausted by refractory disciplinary problems. In personality she scored probably objective, but only three significant responses away from the extremely subjective division. As worksample 35 is inaccurate to this extent, the Laboratory considers it wiser for her to assume herself extremely subjective.

In ideaphoria she scored at the 100th percentile, 460 words written in ten minutes where 341 is grade *A* for women. She wanted to write, but whenever she tried her vivid imagination raced ahead at a speed which her pencil could never equal, and she grew discouraged and gave up.

She then thought of editing a collection of children's stories. This gave the counterfeit satisfaction of having produced something without the long laborious hours demanded by actual creation. But secure editors score highest in the reasoning worksamples, analytical reasoning, worksample 244, and inductive

TABLE XXXVl

A RESTLESS ACCOUNTANT

high (100th percentile)	in accounting aptitude
high (99th percentile)	in ideaphoria
extremely objective	in personality
high (90th percentile)	in abstract visualization
average (40th percentile)	in analytical reasoning
low (10th percentile)	in structural visualization
low (5th percentile)	in inductive reasoning

THESE ARE THE APTITUDE SCORES OF A CERTIFIED PUBLIC ACCOUNTANT WHO ENJOYED HIS WORK SO LONG AS HE COULD AUDIT A NEW ACCOUNT EVERY FEW MONTHS, BUT WHO GREW RESTLESS AND IMPATIENT ON A MORE IMPORTANT ASSIGNMENT WHICH LASTED TWO AND A HALF YEARS.

reasoning, worksample 164, in both of which she scored low. Also editors score lower in ideaphoria, where she ranks at the 100th percentile. Continued editorial work would give her little permanent enjoyment.

College teaching involves fewer disciplinary problems but demands more inductive reasoning than the grades. A change from public to private school seemed likely to give a congenial atmosphere for her subjectivity. But the only enduring solution hopeful of lasting satisfaction is actual creative work. She should force herself to write a regular two hours each day, devoting ten minutes of this period to scribbling at top speed exactly as in the creative-imagination test, worksample 161, where she turned out record production. Instead of throwing away these crude outpourings, like most high creative people, with nothing to show for her efforts, she should bind them carefully in some sort of loose-leaf book, where they will not be lost, and then each day spend the balance of her writing time amending them phrase by phrase, word by word.

With the title of manager in a public accounting firm, a short, thick-set, dynamic man, approaching forty, who paced the floor incessantly as he talked, took over a new problem every two or three months, met a strange group in fresh surroundings, and enjoyed his work. Then, in view of his

TABLE XXXVII

A RESTLESS DENTIST

high (90th percentile)	ideaphoria
high (90th percentile)	tweezer dexterity
high (80th percentile)	structural visualization
extremely subjective	personality
average (50th percentile)	inductive reasoning
low (20th percentile)	abstract visualization

THIS DENTIST CAME TO BE TESTED WITH THE BELIEF THAT HE LACKED ABILITY TO ACQUIRE SKILL. HIS HANDICAP IS HIGH IDEAPHORIA WHICH MAKES HIM PERPETUALLY CHANGE HIS ENVIRONMENT, MOVE HIS INSTRUMENTS, REARRANGE HIS OFFICE, SO THAT HE GIVES HIMSELF NO CHANCE TO ACQUIRE SKILL, WHICH COMES WITH DOING THE SAME THING EVERY DAY IN THE SAME WAY. HE MUST FIND A CONSTRUCTIVE OUTLET FOR THIS CREATIVE IMAGINATION.

recognized ability, he received a more important assignment; and at the end of two and a half years, in one office, handling the same problem, he came to be tested with so keen a distaste for accounting that he wondered if he had ever belonged in the field. He scored as shown in table xxxvi.

His accounting aptitude, abstract visualization, analytical reasoning, and low structural visualization, all combine in accounting. But ideaphoria demands outlet. This he gained for a time through the perpetual shift from one minor accounting job to another, but lost as he rose in responsibility, for top accountants score low.

Venting his 90th percentile ideaphoria, a financially established dentist moved his office incessantly to a new building. When held by a lease, he tore out partitions, redecorated the walls, moved furniture. After each sweeping renovation he announced himself settled for life, but within a year neighbors saw laths and plaster carted away; for dental practice does not ordinarily exhaust a volcanic mind.

The man came with the question: Could the Laboratory measure ability to learn?; for he felt that he had no assured professional skill either in his vocation or at the piano, which he played for pleasure. His trouble is too much ideaphoria, for he alters his methods perpetually, never allowing himself

TABLE XXXVIII

A POTENTIAL NEWSPAPER EDITOR AND COLUMN WRITER

extremely objective	in personality
high (95th percentile)	in abstract visualization
high (95th percentile)	in ideaphoria
high (85th percentile)	in accounting aptitude
low (10th percentile)	in inductive reasoning
low (6th percentile)	in structural visualization
average (60th percentile)	in English vocabulary

EXECUTIVE WORK USES OBJECTIVITY, ABSTRACT VISUALIZATION, AND ACCOUNTING APTITUDE. WRITING USES IDEAPHORIA. EDITORS AS A GROUP AVERAGE HIGH IN INDUCTIVE REASONING, AND NOT SO HIGH IN IDEAPHORIA; BUT FEW INDIVIDUAL EDITORS POSSESS EVERY TRAIT OF THE EDITORIAL GROUP. INTERVIEWERS AND RESEARCHERS AVERAGE HIGH IN IDEAPHORIA, AND NOT SO HIGH IN INDUCTIVE REASONING. IN SOME COMBINATION OF INTERVIEWING AND EDITORIAL EXECUTIVE WORK. EXACTLY THE CAREER WHICH INTERESTED THIS MAN, HE WOULD FIND OUTLET FOR EVERY APTITUDE.

time to acquire the skill he craves, which comes only with repetition. Change anything, adjust the light to a new angle, rearrange the instruments, reorient the patient's chair, and one starts again at the beginning. There is always the danger of lagging behind modern developments through stolid inertia; but one high in creative imagination must guard against the opposite fatiguing tendency, changing so erratically as never to acquire a conditioned reflex. Despite his financial success, and his possession of every dental aptitude, table xxxvii, this man found no natural outlet for his vivid ideaphoria and no satisfying happiness in professional dentistry.

In the light of his own financial prosperity, he considered setting himself up as a business advisor to other members of the profession. This would undoubtedly use ideaphoria, but not his characteristic dental pattern; for advisors in general score in aptitudes like teachers, and not like successful men and women in the fields they are teaching. The administrator suggested the part-time teaching of dentistry, to use ideaphoria and inductive reasoning, and still tax his dental aptitudes by continuing to practice his profession. Others, already tested

TABLE XXXIX

FOUR APTITUDES WHICH MEMBERS OF THE
STAFF BELIEVE FIND OUTLET IN THE
PRACTICE OF DENTISTRY

high	structural visualization
high	tweezer dexterity
extremely subjective	personality
low	ideaphoria

HIGH IDEAPHORIA MAKES A DENTIST RESTLESS AND DISCONTENT WITH HIS WORK, DENTAL PRACTICE NOT ORDINARILY GIVING SUFFICIENT OUTLET TO THIS TRAIT.

by the Laboratory, have found part-time teaching a happy outlet for high, and otherwise idle, ideaphoria.

Wounds which caused a slight limp, together with an arm which seemed at times to dangle loosely at his side, though now and then he used it with surprising skill, prevented a forty-one-year-old army major from returning to dentistry where he earned an excellent living for fifteen years before joining the army. His aptitude pattern, table xxxviii, also militates against a return, for he scores objective in personality in contrast to the dentist's extreme subjectivity, table xxxix, low in structural visualization, and high in ideaphoria. The combination of this last trait with abstract visualization implies writing as an outlet. Extreme objectivity, high ideaphoria, abstract visualization, and low inductive reasoning, mean selling, possibly newspaper interviewing, or more generally some form of group influencing. The selling of dental instruments and supplies would use this man's aptitudes and to some extent his acquired knowledge, but would not be congenial to a former member of the profession and unsuitable to one as high as the 60th percentile in English vocabulary. A sales executive position would use this vocabulary, but not his interests.

The teaching of dentistry would use his high ideaphoria, usually idle and often disturbing in dental practice. A community project, the organization of a dental clinic, would give him a chance to teach subordinates, to educate the community in better dental care, and to influence public opinion more than

TABLE XL

TRAITS USED IN SALES PROMOTING

high	ideaphoria
objective	personality
high	abstract visualization
high or average	inductive reasoning
high or average	analytical reasoning
low	structural visualization

THESE SAME TRAITS ARE USED IN ALL GROUP-INFLUENCING ACTIVITIES WHICH INVOLVE TEACHING, SUCH AS ADVERTISING AND PUBLIC HEALTH.

as a private practitioner, and would use the aptitudes of table XL, the ideal pattern of the born teacher, inductive reasoning and analytical reasoning added to the salesman's traits.

At this point in the discussion the man asked to return to the earlier mention of writing and newspaper work; and for the first time said that his family owned and operated a newspaper syndicate. His first ambition was to run a daily column, based on interviewing celebrities, a perfect challenge for his total aptitude pattern; but his older brother had gone into the newspaper business and the family thought it wise for the younger son to turn elsewhere.

Among time-wasting hobbies, which dissipate priceless aptitudes, a constructive exception is creative writing started as an avocation and gradually established, the owner of ideaphoria meanwhile earning a living wage in some remote calling. A baker's assistant, with the ideal writing pattern, table XLI, voiced a craving to express himself in print; but salable copy requires both the essential aptitudes and nice word knowledge, where this man scored low. While English vocabulary is obtainable, and such an aptitude pattern encourages its acquisition, this oven tender will undoubtedly turn back, disheartened by the inexhaustible hours of hard labor expended in scaling so hazy a height, for he has no friends to encourage him over sheer head walls. Granted the aptitudes of the writer, with some chance of the pen as a gainful vocation, a man should keep to his own intimate

TABLE XLI

Aptitudes Used in Creative Writing

high	ideaphoria
high	abstract visualization
extremely subjective	personality
low	structural visualization
low	accounting aptitude

TO APPLY THIS APTITUDE PATTERN PRACTICALLY IN EARNING A LIVING DEMANDS AN EXACT KNOWLEDGE OF THE NICE MEANINGS OF ENGLISH WORDS.

experiences; writing to escape life is a legitimate privilege only for one who regards it as an indulgent pastime. Even where work and avocation conflict a man who writes of his own occupation gains unexpected pleasure from its history, modern techniques, and probable future, while his authoritative writing carries more weight than exotic descriptions of a world he has not yet seen.

Success in life does not come plainly, marked by chiseled milestones. Years later, historians discern in retrospect a decisive turning point with artificial clarity, picking some minor incident, single battle, or technical advance, which at the time seemed no more than another link in an endless concatenation of events. Could the Laboratory say with confidence: one more year will bring recognition, it might go far toward strengthening single-minded persistence. Sometimes a crystallizing of confidence carries success. A clearly predominant aptitude for a popular vocation, structural visualization or accounting aptitude, leaves no alternative, though success comes more slowly than hoped; but ideaphoria alone, or several competing aptitudes, drives a man restlessly, seeking success ready made, missing it repeatedly, shifting his main course just before he reaches the vital blind turning.

VIII

FORESIGHT

Worksample 307, originally called VISUAL IMAGINATION, was designed to replace worksample 161, the current measure of creative imagination, now too much affected by writing speed; attempts to measure this last factor separately and then to correct for its presence have not as yet proved sound. But the new worksample 307, visual imagination, and worksample 161, creative imagination, correlate only 0.14, showing the two tests to be virtually independent. The new test is not therefore an improvement over the earlier worksample 161, but an indication of a distinct characteristic.

Each black arrowhead of figure 7 marks the separately determined median of a different age. The figure shows men and women combined, for previous study revealed no sex difference. Unlike most aptitudes, which mature before 20, scores in worksample 307 improve to the age of 28. For age 9, at the extreme left, the median is 45; for age 10, the median is 37; for age 11, 40. These disjoined points jump about due to small populations for some ages, but in general rise as shown by the smooth curve drawn amongst them.

Figure 8 plots in a similar manner the seventy-fifth percentile for each age and the smoothed curve through them; while figure 9 gathers together on one graph three important curves, the twenty-fifth percentile at the bottom, with the seventy-fifth percentile taken directly from figure 8 at the top. The median points, from figure 7, show their scatter in relation to the total vertical spread. The curves have been drawn so that throughout their entire lengths the ratio between the median and the seventy-fifth percentile is always the same. This is true also of the ratio between the median and the twenty-fifth percentile. Figure 10, based on a population of 2101 persons of both sexes, shows the distribution of their scores, corrected to the adult plateau.

The late maturing, age 28, suggests that cultivated knowledge permeates the outcome. On the other hand, these age curves level off like an indigenous aptitude. The conflicting

FIGURE 7

GROWTH WITH AGE OF VISUAL IMAGINATION, FORESIGHT — MEASURED BY WORKSAMPLE 307

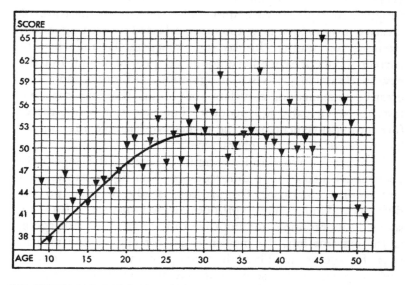

THE BOTTOM POINT OF EACH ARROW SHOWS THE MEDIAN FOR EACH AGE. THE
HEAVY LINE, RISING FROM 37 AT AGE 9 TO A PLATEAU AT A SCORE OF 52,
SHOWS THE PROBABLE GROWTH ON THE ASSUMPTION THAT THE SEPARATE
MEDIANS JUMP AROUND ONLY BECAUSE OF SMALL POPULATIONS FOR THE
SEPARATE AGES. TOTAL POPULATION 2,116 PERSONS.

implications of late maturing and final plateau led to a painstaking mathematical study of the relation between distribution curves for different ages, the final statistical distinction
between an inherent aptitude and acquired knowledge.

Originally the Laboratory held that every aptitude ought
to show a sex difference, but abandoned this notion when it
isolated personality and tonal memory, which behave like
aptitudes but where men and women score the same. With
the appearance of the bimodal curve for personality and the
gradual association of aptitudes with genes, the idea now pre-
vails that only those aptitudes which arise from the X chromo-
some, about one in twenty-four, differ with men and women.

FIGURE 8

CHANGE WITH AGE OF THE 75TH PERCENTILE
FOR VISUAL IMAGINATION — FORESIGHT

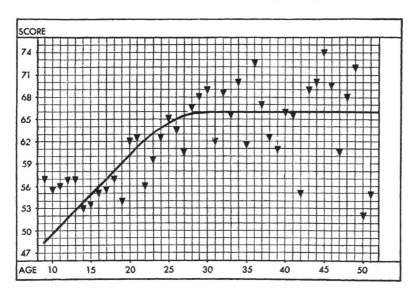

THE BLACK LINE, RISING FROM JUST BELOW 50 AT AGE 10 TO THE ADULT
PLATEAU AT A SCORE OF 66, SHOWS PROBABLE IMPROVEMENT WITH AGE.
SCORES ABOVE THE BLACK LINE THE LABORATORY CONSIDERS IN THE TOP
QUARTER FOR EACH AGE, GRADE A.

The age curve for observation, which matures rapidly to
18 with boys and starts down as early as 27, throws doubt
on the significance of the adult plateau as an essential criterion
of an aptitude. This leaves only the mathematical relation of
one age to another. With worksample 307 the distribution
curve for any age, multiplied by the proper factor, reproduces
the corresponding distribution for any other age. This never
occurs with knowledge tests, where learning intervenes between one age and another and destroys the simple mathematical relationship. This suggests that worksample 307 measures a new aptitude, and not knowledge despite the late
maturing, important in light of the next step, the validation,
which once more makes the outcome seem like knowledge,

FIGURE 9

COMPARISON OF 75TH, 50TH, AND 25TH PERCENTILE
GROWTH CURVES FOR VISUAL IMAGINATION

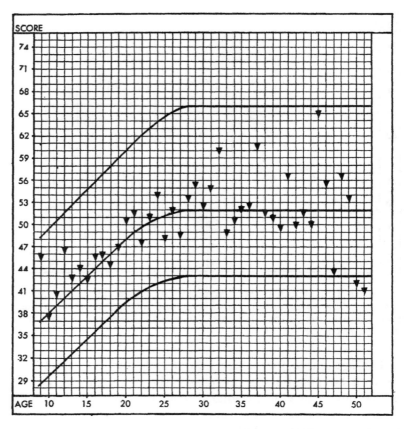

THE BOTTOM POINT OF EACH ARROW IS THE SEPARATELY DETERMINED MEDIAN
FOR EACH AGE COPIED EXACTLY FROM FIGURE 7 TOGETHER WITH THE MIDDLE
BLACK LINE. THE UPPER LINE, WHICH PARALLELS IT, IS THE 75TH PERCENTILE
FROM FIGURE 8. THUS TWENTY-FIVE PERCENTILES SEPARATE THESE LINES.
SCORES BETWEEN THESE LINES THE LABORATORY CALLS GRADE B. THE BOTTOM
LINE IS THE 25TH PERCENTILE, TWENTY-FIVE PERCENTILES BELOW THE MEDIAN.
ALTHOUGH THE INDIVIDUALLY DETERMINED MEDIANS OF FIGURE 7 SEEM TO
VARY ERRATICALLY, MANY OF THEM ARE WITHIN TEN PERCENTILES OF THE
SMOOTHED MEDIAN LINE. THESE THREE CURVES ALL LEVEL OFF INTO THE ADULT
PLATEAU AT THE SAME POINT, AGE 28. THIS IS CHARACTERISTIC OF ALL APTI-
TUDE CURVES THUS FAR PLOTTED, AND DIFFERENTIATES APTITUDES FROM GRIP.

FIGURE 10

VISUAL IMAGINATION — FORESIGHT
DISTRIBUTION OF WORKSAMPLE 307 FORM AA

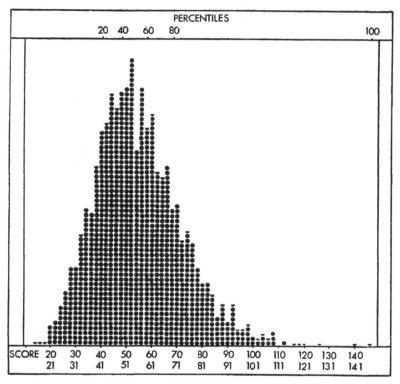

THIS FIGURE SHOWS THE DISTRIBUTION OF 2101 INDIVIDUAL SCORES, CONVERTED
MATHEMATICALLY TO THE ADULT PLATEAU. IT INCLUDES BOTH MEN AND
WOMEN, SINCE THERE SEEMS TO BE NO DIFFERENCE BETWEEN THE SEXES.
DIRECTLY BELOW THE FIGURE 20 AT THE TOP, UNDER THE HEADING PERCEN-
TILES, IS THE SCORE OF 41 AT THE BOTTOM, INDICATING THAT 20 PER CENT
OF ADULTS SCORE 41 OR LESS. BELOW THE 80TH PERCENTILE IS THE SCORE 69.

The established professions appear more frequently among
the vocations of adults high in worksample 307 than in a
parallel column based on low grades. But a tabulation of all
tested professional people compared with others, the next
step in the validation study, failed to confirm this first indication. After several vain attempts to subdivide professional

workers, research stumbled on a class of persons who grade
A in worksample 307 more often than *D*, men and women
in work which demands unremunerative years of formal training. This includes lawyers and physicians, but not engineers,
for here some men still attain the top through practical
experience. Certified public accountants score high, but not
accountants in general. Unskilled laborers score low.

At one stage business executives seemed to score high in
worksample 307; but more careful analysis shows this to apply
only to men who develop their own business, while executives of similar rank who work for a steady salary score low.

A high score in worksample 307 seems to reveal an intellectual vision of a remote goal, foresight. a gift for seeing
far ahead the worth of professional training, or the value of
immediate financial sacrifice in order to gain the remote
satisfaction of controlling an enterprise.

IX

INDUCTIVE REASONING

With elder brothers in the United States Navy, a high-
school stripling ran away from home in the middle of his
sophomore year and joined the merchant marine. After a
round of fist fights, and subsequent reprimands, he landed
in jail. Six months later his parole officer sent him to be tested,
paying the fee. for he had no appropriate drawing fund.

Inductive reasoning at the 100th percentile, table XLII, signi-
fies a phenomenal speed and accuracy in intellectual reasoning;
low structural visualization and its complement, high abstract
visualization, imply the handling of ideas, not things. But
neither inductive reasoning nor abstract visualization can be
utilized without words; and the combination when idle means
dumb frustration. With this explanation, the youth brandished
his clenched fist and said he talked with that. In terms of aptitude measurements he thinks as correctly as anyone who has
tried the inductive-reasoning worksample; but he has no adequate words in which to formulate his disembodied thoughts
and convey them to others. At the age of seventeen he had

been in jail, deprived of his seaman's papers, and robbed of many citizenship privileges; his only fault is an unfulfilled craving for peaceful expression.

On delivering his chubby, smiling, twelve-year-old son to the Laboratory a Connecticut lawyer alleged that his own

TABLE XLII

TEST SCORES OF A BOY PAROLED FROM A REFORMATORY

high (100th percentile)	inductive reasoning
high (95th percentile)	abstract visualization
high (75th percentile)	analytical reasoning
average (50th percentile)	creative imagination
average (45th percentile)	accounting aptitude
low (30th percentile)	pitch discrimination
low (20th percentile)	tonal memory
low (15th percentile)	number memory
low (6th percentile)	structural visualization
low (20th percentile)	English vocabulary

BECAUSE THIS BOY LACKS WORDS TO EXPRESS HIS TOP THREE APTITUDES, HE TRIED TO WIN ARGUMENTS WITH HIS FISTS AND LANDED IN JAIL.

father, the boy's grandfather. had studied engineering but never used it; his grandfather, the boy's great grandfather, after studying law, had never passed the bar examinations; while the great, great grandfather graduated in medicine but never practiced. The father questioned his own fitness for law and continued only because of the financial impracticability of fresh experimenting. After four generations of false starts and abortive indecisions the father promised his son every discriminative aid in the scientific choice of a life's work.

The boy scored high inductive reasoning and low accounting aptitude, a divergent pair certain to pull in conflict; for low accounting aptitude makes high-school assignments long and laborious, so that a boy alters restlessly his curriculum groping for some easy course. He drops Latin for a year, but never returns, and thereafter finds an exact English vocabulary just out of reach; but law, teaching, writing, diplomacy, international relations, diagnostic medicine, research science, which use inductive reasoning, all require wide and scrupulous vocabularies. None of the three aptitudes: abstract visualization, inductive reasoning, and analytical reasoning, can be used without words, which are the tools of abstract thinking. This low-accounting-aptitude boy faces exactly the future

TABLE XLIII

An Aptitude Pattern which Creates a Conflict Between Intellectual Work and Manual Operations

high (90th percentile)	abstract visualization
high (80th percentile)	inductive reasoning
high (80th percentile)	finger dexterity
high (80th percentile)	tweezer dexterity
extremely subjective	personality
average (50th percentile)	visual imagination (foresight)
low (11th percentile)	structural visualization
low (25th percentile)	English vocabulary

COULD THIS SERVICE MAN FOLLOW HIS YOUTHFUL AMBITION FOR INTERNATIONAL LAW HE WOULD USE MOST OF HIS APTITUDES: ABSTRACT VISUALIZATION, INDUCTIVE REASONING, AND EXTREME SUBJECTIVITY. BUT HIS HIGH FINGER AND TWEEZER DEXTERITIES MAKE IT TOO EASY FOR HIM TO EARN AN ADEQUATE LIVING AT SOME MANUAL OPERATION; AND WITH ONLY AVERAGE FORESIGHT HE WILL FIND IT VERY DIFFICULT TO CONTINUE EDUCATION LONG ENOUGH TO GAIN THE REQUISITE KNOWLEDGE.

his father fears. His only hope is to recognize candidly his academic difficulties, continue Latin no matter how troublesome, and gain a precise knowledge of the English language, without which he can never use his aptitude pattern.

After four and a half years with the armed services a man of twenty-eight scored as shown in table XLIII. He will probably apply his finger and tweezer dexterities to repetitive factory assembly, the easy choice. Because of extreme subjectivity, he is unlikely to advance to an executive position, and will not enjoy it if he does, and because of low structural visualization he will likewise never gain the top of a mechanical trade. He had in fact started factory assembly, using his finger dexterity, but saw that it offered him nothing he valued. During his army life he spent hours in reading international relations, diplomacy, history, and government. He chose friends from the intellectual professions; but with meager education he had no criterion for evaluating his obscure cravings.

In the interpretation of a bargraph, no aptitude is more important than another; either the dexterities or the reasonings when idle cause restlessness. But a forced choice between the two tempts one to neglect the former in favor of the latter. Extreme subjectivity denotes a profession, high abstract visualization and low structural visualization one which deals with ideas, not with things, while inductive reasoning approximates legal thinking. But jurisprudence is a high-vocabulary profession and, while theoretically attainable, a long, arduous climb from this man's eighth-grade education and 25th percentile English vocabulary. His prospects in international law are remote and visionary; but the Laboratory can state the situation with surprising clarity. The man has exactly the aptitudes for his ambition, and with courage, perseverance, and the strength demanded by long hours of study, his lack of knowledge is remediable. While unnaturally quiet the man radiated an irresistible charm and, with the total situation clearly stated, the Laboratory has seen men overcome apparently insurmountable obstacles. The danger is that he may see the attractive distance momentarily with intellectual perspicuity by inductive reasoning but lack the natural foresight to persist; for in worksample 307, which measures a gift for holding a desirable goal persistently in mind, he scores only at the 50th percentile, low in comparison with his other aptitudes.

A girl four years younger, with almost the same aptitudes, table XLIV, rejected law unequivocally, for her low accounting aptitude and low vocabulary combined prejudiced her unreasonably against further education. Her expressed interest centered somewhere in the theatrical world. In acting she would undoubtedly use her extremely subjective personality; but this was not her goal. She responded to the lighting effects of the theater, its excitement, constantly changing population, and romance. Inductive reasoning she would use in gaining coherence in writing, and with more words, which the Laboratory urged, she may discover playwrighting. She mentioned directing, in which she had some amateur experience. Inductive reasoning, her top trait, is second in order of importance among teachers; and the teaching aspects of handling a theatrical troop may attract her. The Laboratory's fear is her low ideaphoria, usually desirable in the theater world. Her

TABLE XLIV

APTITUDES OF A WOMAN INTERESTED IN THE THEATER

extremely subjective	personality
(2 significant responses on forms AE and FK)	
high (80th percentile)	inductive reasoning
average (55th percentile)	abstract visualization
average (46th percentile)	structural visualization
low (30th percentile)	ideaphoria
low (20th percentile)	accounting aptitude
low (25th percentile)	English vocabulary

PRESUMABLY THIS APTITUDE PATTERN WOULD FIND COMPLETE OUTLET IN LAW; BUT ITS POSSESSOR IS INTERESTED IN THE THEATER. SHE WOULD USE HER PERSONALITY, INDUCTIVE REASONING, AND ABSTRACT VISUALIZATION, IN DRAMATIC CRITICISM AND PLAYWRIGHTING, BUT FOR TOP ACHIEVEMENT CREATIVE WRITING SOMETIMES DEMANDS IDEAPHORIA AS WELL.

interest in the Thespian scene may be real and should be used as a vital incentive to read plays, study stage techniques, dramatic histories and criticisms; for without more knowledge her top three traits: extreme subjectivity, inductive reasoning, and abstract visualization, are disturbing adjuncts.

An extremely subjective, abnormally retarded, fifteen-year-old boy, within a few days of his sixteenth birthday, and still in eighth grade, scored uniformly left eyed in worksample 236, which, with the use of the right hand, so often leads to reading difficulties and a low vocabulary. His parents believed him ambidextrous; but adopting advice received five years earlier from another authority, to pick one hand only in preference to the other, they had chosen the right. He could not read the simplest vocabulary test, and when it was read aloud scored low. Despite three years' retardation in school and reading inability, combined with unnaturally low accounting aptitude, the boy scored high in the inductive-reasoning worksample. The mother construed the problem: could her son not equip his one brilliant asset with the requisite words he would go through life, as she expressed it, by brute force and awkwardness.

TABLE XLV

A POTENTIAL MUSIC CRITIC

high (100th percentile)	tonal memory
high (98th percentile)	inductive reasoning
high (93d percentile)	analytical reasoning
high (90th percentile)	pitch discrimination
probably objective	personality
(20 significant responses on the combined forms AE and FJ)	
low (20th percentile)	English vocabulary
low (15th percentile)	structural visualization
low (15th percentile)	finger dexterity
low (10th percentile)	observation
low (10th percentile)	ideaphoria
low (5th percentile)	accounting aptitude

MUSICAL CRITICISM DID NOT SEEM VIRILE ENOUGH TO THIS MAN UNTIL HE HAD FAILED AT SELLING AND AT BOTH MECHANICAL AND CLERICAL JOBS.

But the father considered a small private school, which the Laboratory felt offered the only just hope, as too expensive; and in addition he wanted the boy at home. Testing a child. and later a mature man with similar aptitudes, the Laboratory sees the future more transparently than parents. Yet it can no more than make its simple recommendations, in this instance a small, recently founded school, more intensive use of the left hand, and specific English vocabulary building.

A thick-set. unkempt. red-haired youth of twenty-two, after scoring below the 5th percentile in accounting aptitude, asked MUSICAL irritably if all examiners were young girls, con- CRITICISM veying the impression that he blamed his low scores on the administrator. When a second structural test confirmed his grade D on the first, he made other disparaging remarks. At the end of his second appointment his complete pattern stood as shown in table XLV. Tonal memory and pitch discrimination together demand musical expression, but not probably in concert performing because of low finger dexterity. Brilliant inductive reasoning, with analytical reasoning added, coupled with low ideaphoria, mean critical writing. From the negative viewpoint, low accounting aptitude shows that he does not belong in an ordinary office job, low structural visualization not in a typical mechanical job, and low ideaphoria not in sales work. In place of the anticipated sarcastic response to this summary, the man commented, almost to himself, that he had tried all three, clerical work, mechanical, and sales, as well as taxi driving and going to sea, just to escape himself; but it was no good. An abiding monopolizing interest in music followed him everywhere; but he was aware of his own inadequate background. In English vocabulary he scored low, at the 20th percentile; but rigidly controlled experiments indicate that vocabulary can be acquired. Could this man have expended the same time and energy in building his vocabulary, and with it his knowledge of music and experience in writing, which he has squandered in worldly directions, he would have risen high in musical criticism.

A returning soldier, with no work experience previous to the war, scored as shown in table XLVI. Ignoring for the moment tonal memory at the top, the next three traits,

extremely subjective	personality,
high	accounting aptitude,
high	analytical reasoning,

form the ideal pattern needed in certified public accounting; for this man probably as good a choice as any among the recognized vocations. But accounting offers little prospect of using either tonal memory or rhythm memory; nor is the accompanying training and experience useful in any direction touching his total pattern.

Starting again with tonal memory as a nucleus, professional music would combine tonal memory, rhythm memory, and extreme subjectivity. Editorial work uses analytical reasoning, ideaphoria, and inductive reasoning. A combination of music and writing, musical criticism or editorial work in music, comes close; musical composing nearer still because it seems to use structural visualization.

With a pattern of this kind the Laboratory can name specific jobs each of which uses two or three aptitudes from the total.

TABLE XLVI

APTITUDES OF A RETURNING SOLDIER

high (100th percentile)	tonal memory
extremely subjective	personality
(2 significant responses on form AE)	
high (93d percentile)	accounting aptitude
high (85th percentile)	analytical reasoning
high (80th percentile)	rhythm memory
average (60th percentile)	structural visualization
average (60th percentile)	ideaphoria
average (55th percentile)	inductive reasoning
average (50th percentile)	foresight

CERTIFIED PUBLIC ACCOUNTING USES HIGH ACCOUNTING APTITUDE, ANALYTICAL REASONING, AND EXTREME SUBJECTIVITY. EDITORIAL WRITING USES ANALYTICAL REASONING, INDUCTIVE REASONING, AND IDEAPHORIA. MUSICAL CRITICISM WOULD USE THIS COMPLETE PATTERN, EXCEPT FOR STRUCTURAL VISUALIZATION. IF PRESENT, MUSICAL COMPOSING COMBINED WITH CRITICISM MIGHT USE IT.

But no named job uses the array; for the world does not bother with a name unless applicable to several hundred, perhaps thousands, of persons. Not enough have this man's pattern. No one yet understands its complete integration.

Having lost precious time through his war service, he felt that he should abandon any idea of aiming high and get back into civilian life quickly, trying merely to earn an ordinary living. Grasping the immediate, in place of the more desirable ultimate, tempts everyone, but is less likely to attract those who score high in worksample 307, visual imagination, intellectual vision, or foresight. This soldier scored at the 50th percentile, probably high enough under normal conditions to hold to his vision; but his extremely high other aptitudes make his foresight low by comparison and though he saw the distant future he felt that he would not arrive.

Any extremely subjective person, high in both accounting aptitude and abstract visualization, but low in English vocabulary, can start as an office clerk and, with new words, advance to bookkeeper, and thence to accountant. But low vocabulary jobs which use inductive reasoning, coupled with abstract visualization, and which lead to advancement, are exceedingly rare. An unusual garage mechanic, whose primary function is the diagnosis of engine troubles, exercises inductive reasoning; but he scores low in structural visualization and has little prospect of promotion.

Detective work is one of the few excellent starts for one with inductive reasoning, although for success this requires more general knowledge than is ordinarily possessed by one low in vocabulary. A United States mail clerk, behind the parcel post window for eight years, scored high in inductive reasoning, high in analytical reasoning, and high in observation, characteristics found among news commentators, top-rank reporters, and so-called magazine researchers, but the man had only an eighth-grade education. In English vocabulary he scores as high as the average college graduate; but in his own words: That would be hard to put over to anyone else. After a number of ridiculously impractical suggestions from the test administrator, the man himself mentioned postal inspection, where intelligent investigation would use inductive reasoning and observation, and where the couching of reports would use analytical reasoning and his large vocabulary, a perfect solution, which demonstrates the importance of each examinee analyzing his own aptitude pattern, for no laboratory can know intimately the postal service and its opportunities, as well as every other modern and coming vocation.

Advertising sales demands abstract visualization and its complement, low structural visualization, together with ideaphoria and inductive reasoning, exactly the aptitudes, table XLVII, of an assured man of thirty-eight who for a number of years had successfully sold advertising space. In addition he had no other disturbing trait apt to engender failure if left idle, his sole departure from the perfect advertising pattern his extreme subjectivity. He came to be tested before accepting an advance position which entailed advising and training salesmen, planning and creating ideas, consulting with the sales staff in place of actual selling. As he described it, this seemed even more suitable to his total pattern. Advisory work is usually subjective. In direct selling, ideaphoria dominates the two reasonings; while in planning, inductive reasoning or analytical

TABLE XLVII

APTITUDE SCORES OF A MAN WHO SELLS
ADVERTISING SUCCESSFULLY

extremely subjective   in personality
(3 significant responses in forms AE and FJ combined)
high (85th percentile)   abstract visualization
high (80th percentile)   inductive reasoning
high (75th percentile)   analytical reasoning
average (70th percentile)   ideaphoria
average (50th percentile)   accounting aptitude
low (20th percentile)   observation
low (16th percentile)   structural visualization
low (15th percentile)   tonal memory
low (10th percentile)   pitch discrimination

IN SELLING ADVERTISING THIS MAN USES IDEAPHORIA, ABSTRACT VISUALIZATION, LOW STRUCTURAL VISUALIZATION, AND HIS AVERAGE ACCOUNTING APTITUDE. HE HANDLES THE SAME LARGE ACCOUNTS YEAR AFTER YEAR, WHICH SUITS HIS EXTREME SUBJECTIVITY. IN PLANNING SALES CAMPAIGNS HE USES INDUCTIVE REASONING AND ANALYTICAL REASONING.

reasoning, in both of which this man excelled, must control ideaphoria. There seemed every reason for this man consenting to merited promotion and it was some time before he revealed his justified worry. His happy independence in the handling of customer accounts, like running his own small business, with only a secretary as an assistant, suited his extreme subjectivity. The new duties involved managing a large department, supervising artists, statisticians, interviewers, and clerks, and he prudently feared these executive functions, which take objectivity, low ideaphoria, and often low inductive reasoning, as opposed to his own high scores. But in at least two recent instances the Laboratory has known comfortable top executives who score extremely subjective and high in ideaphoria, one the general superintendent of a chemical plant, the other president of a textile mill, both of whom successfully developed subordinates to run the executive details. If this man becomes a department head in actual function he will probably fail. If on the other

TABLE XLVIII

TAXATION LAW OR PURE MATHEMATICS

extremely subjective	in personality
high	in abstract visualization
average (70th percentile)	in inductive reasoning
average (70th percentile)	in accounting aptitude
low	in analytical reasoning
low	in structural visualization
low (20th percentile)	in English vocabulary

THIS MAN'S EXTREME SUBJECTIVITY SUGGESTS A PROFESSION. INDUCTIVE REA-SONING SUGGESTS LAW. ACCOUNTING APTITUDE SUGGESTS ACCOUNTING. SOME COMBINATION OF LAW AND ACCOUNTING, AS TAXATION LAW, MIGHT USE ALL THREE. STATISTICAL RESEARCH, PURE MATHEMATICS, OR WRITING ON MATHE-MATICS, MIGHT GIVE EQUAL OUTLET.

hand he can plan sales campaigns, train and inspire the sales staff, and develop a congenial subordinate to administer the daily routine, he has every chance of brilliant success.

Certified public accounting would use the 70th-percentile accounting aptitude, extreme subjectivity, abstract visualization, and low structural visualization, table XLVIII, of a rough but attractive man, honorably discharged after three and a half years of military service. Inductive reasoning and ana-lytical reasoning often seem interchangeable in life, except that accountants score generally high in analytical reasoning, not necessarily in inductive reasoning. Law would use inductive reasoning, extreme subjectivity, and again the complementary pair, abstract visualization and low structural visualization. Some combination of law and accounting, such as taxation law, approaches a complete challenge; or, because inductive reasoning characterizes the scientist who formulates a law, statistical research would probably challenge the same aptitude pattern, accounting aptitude in numerical manipulation and inductive reasoning in the formulation of general laws.

Were the world's occupations limited to law and medicine, the Laboratory would certainly hesitate in suggesting the avoidance of either; but with legions of widely diverse pursuits ahead of modern youth, the legal profession, where one competes with thousands going in the same direction, seems a needless risk, unless one happens to have, with considerable certainty, the legal aptitudes. At the end of twelve years in law, and four years after his father's death, an extremely subjective man gave up his law office and came to be tested, declaring that he had failed. His subjectivity indicated a profession. But in structural visualization he scored at the 58th percentile, above the theoretical 51st, which indicates its full presence. A man with structural visualization does not belong in law, which requires the complementary abstract visualization; but governed by this man's structural scores alone, within eight percentiles of the crucial point, no administrator would dare advise against a father's profession.

Coupled with this he scored at the 85th percentile in English vocabulary, ordinarily high enough to succeed in any direction, without the corresponding aptitudes. But his low, 10th-percentile, inductive reasoning, apparently synonymous with legal reasoning, and possibly high structural visualization, overcame his vocabulary and the enviable asset of a flourishing inherited practice.

Seldom should low inductive reasoning alone keep an extremely subjective man or woman out of law, for legal training leads to an invaluable background, and high English vocabulary; but one already high in vocabulary, with low inductive reasoning, should investigate alternatives.

Lack of inductive reasoning worries every person who scores low in worksample 164. An extremely subjective high-school boy, table XLIX, who had read no brochure in advance and so came unprepared, wasted much of his appointment time in arguing about his low, 30th-percentile, inductive-reasoning score, and meanwhile missed three vital points: his extreme subjectivity, which he recognized as a correct expression of himself and yet he had thought of business; his unmistakable left eyedness in worksample 236, for he used his right hand; and his abstract visualization and low structural visualization.

Inductive reasoning is desirable in critical writing, diagnostic medicine, editorial work, law. and teaching, although even here not always essential. It may influence general thinking more than other aptitudes. With one man who scored below the 5th percentile the effect of low inductive reasoning showed in

TABLE XLIX

A HIGH-SCHOOL BOY TROUBLED BY HIS
LOW INDUCTIVE-REASONING SCORE

extremely subjective	personality
high (85th percentile)	abstract visualization
high	memory for design
low (30th percentile)	inductive reasoning
left	eyedness
high (95th percentile)	English vocabulary

THIS BOY BELONGS IN A PROFESSION DEALING WITH IDEAS. HE SHOULD BEGIN CAUTIOUSLY TO LEARN NEW THINGS WITH HIS LEFT HAND. HE SHOULD GAIN ENOUGH KNOWLEDGE OF ART TO BE PREPARED TO USE MEMORY FOR DESIGN. THESE FINDINGS ARE MORE VITAL THAN HIS 30TH-PERCENTILE INDUCTIVE REASONING WHICH HE INSISTED ON DISCUSSING AT THE EXPENSE OF EVERYTHING ELSE. HE HAD SCORED HIGH IN PREVIOUS REASONING TESTS, TAKEN IN SCHOOL, AND COULD NOT UNDERSTAND HIS LOW SCORE IN WORKSAMPLE 164.

a slowness in grasping instructions, in interpreting scores, and in applying the separate results to his own problem. But lack of the trait does not preclude success. Furthermore, it can be replaced in life by analytical reasoning, perhaps a distinct aptitude, a gift for arranging facts, for organizing material, compared with inductive reasoning, a gift for sensing an obscure relationship. for seeing a common element or idea.

One who scores low in both inductive reasoning and analytical reasoning should replace this aptitude with knowledge, which assures a tried decision, for countless recurrent situations have been met before and the right course determined by centuries of experimentation. While one who scores high can instinctively chance a snap decision, one low should never jump impetuously to a conclusion, but reason slowly and consciously, striving perpetually to know instantly the correct course vindicated by accumulated knowledge.

x

NUMBER MEMORY

The gawky, disheveled son of an eminent Boston father loves geography, knows by name every battlefield in the world war, innumerable tiny towns on the perpetually changing world fronts; and yet he seems woefully feeble-minded. At twenty he graduated from high school, with the recommendation that he take up farming. To the urban-bred teacher the raising of poultry, specifically mentioned, seems a menial job within the mental capabilities of one three or four years retarded; but the boy scores highest in number memory and extremely subjective. Only at some professional level can this type of personality gain lasting happiness. The objective man, who scores low in structural visualization, can make poultry raising a profitable business by effective selling; the high structural, extremely subjective man can run it as a highly scientific enterprise; but one who scores extremely subjective and low in structural visualization is unhappy in business and equally unhappy in science, with little chance of using number memory, when this represents his top trait, as shown in the form of a bargraph, figure 11.

Final graduation from high school, and the understanding attention of a senior teacher, had given the boy a pleasant confidence which the father feared to jeopardize. But stopping further education is too drastic a price; for the boy will fail at poultry farming, with consequences more devastating than low marks in school. This boy's father and mother are still young, and financially able to pay for additional academic background. The Laboratory believes it wiser for such a boy to experiment during his father's life rather than unaided later. In measurable terms he needs English vocabulary more than farming experience. If practical necessities force him later into a field where he belongs as little as in poultry growing he will be more successful for added knowledge.

In answer to the mother's assertion that her son scored low in general intelligence, and so should not continue with education, the Laboratory finds no supporting evidence for

FIGURE 11

BARGRAPH OF BOY HIGHEST IN NUMBER MEMORY

APTITUDE MEASURED	WORKSAMPLE NUMBER	LETTER GRADE				PERCENTILE
		D	C	B	A	
Number Memory	165					91
Finger Dexterity	16					70
Proportion Appraisal	235B					65
Accounting Aptitude	268					45
Analytical Reasoning	244					45
Inductive Reasoning	164					42
Observation	206					32
Structural Visualization	5					25
Tonal Memory	365					20
Pitch Discrimination	364					20
Creative Imagination	161					17
Tweezer Dexterity	18					15
Vocabulary	176BA					5
Objectivity	35AE					5
Memory for Design	294					1

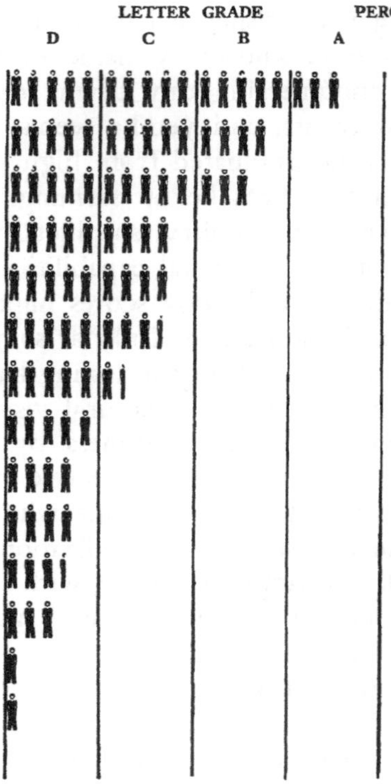

IN NUMBER MEMORY THIS BOY SCORES HIGHER THAN 90 PER CENT OF OTHERS HIS AGE, AS SHOWN GRAPHICALLY BY THE LENGTH OF THE TOP LINE OF EIGHTEEN LITTLE FIGURES, WHICH EXTENDS INTO THE A QUARTILE. IN OBJECTIVITY HE SCORES AT THE 5TH PERCENTILE. THIS MEANS THAT WERE HIS EXTREME SUBJECTIVITY PLOTTED IT WOULD BE AT THE 95TH PERCENTILE. BECAUSE OF AVERAGE ACCOUNTING APTITUDE, THE BOY BELONGS IN A MEDIUM SIZED SCHOOL, BECAUSE OF LOW VOCABULARY IN ONE RECENTLY FOUNDED; FOR HE MUST GET MORE KNOWLEDGE DEMANDED BY HIS SUBJECTIVITY.

the prevalent feeling that a scholastically handicapped boy strikes an academic ceiling beyond which he climbs no higher. Countless boys, low in accounting aptitude and low in English vocabulary, cease to learn new words, standing still year after year; and, since the same combination leads to low general-intelligence scores, one naturally assumes that low intelligence limits learning. But the Laboratory has seen numerous such boys, placed in small, recently founded schools, advance as rapidly from their own levels as high-accounting-aptitude, high-vocabulary companions. Boys stand still only when the class average, the level of instruction, is beyond or below their own knowledge boundary. This mother felt that her son's survival depended upon her constant push, for he showed no scholastic drive of his own. Except for rare instances the low-accounting-aptitude, low-vocabulary boy shows no enthusiasm in a large school; and this boy had never experienced the small, intimate student body.

With an objective boy, high number memory suggests scheduling, routing, production control in manufacturing, or stockroom keeping, as effective avenues toward supervision; but for one who scores extremely subjective, who does not belong in the objective industrial world, they represent dead ends. An extremely subjective boy or girl should seek from the outset a congenial environment, although vastly harder to find than a business or industrial position.

A stocky boy scored 18 significant responses on the combined forms AE and FJ, in the extremely subjective division but so close to the critical point between 18 and 19 that no experienced administrator has confidence in the classification. In addition he scored highest, at the 78th percentile, in number memory; equally high in pitch discrimination; at the 40th percentile in accounting aptitude; very low, 10th percentile, in structural visualization; average, 45th percentile, in vocabulary; and low, 10th percentile, in creative imagination, inductive reasoning, and observation. For this combination of aptitudes the Laboratory has no practical advice.

After two appointments of three hours each this freckle-faced boy understood clearly the known significance of each aptitude and saw the Laboratory's inability to give inclusive advice based on the total pattern. But the father, who had taken no tests himself, and who had read no brochure, was loud in his condemnation of an organization which, as he expressed it, accepted money and gave nothing in return. The Laboratory measured this boy's aptitudes with known accu-

racy. It told him as much about each aptitude separately as is
known. But of the several hundred thousand ways in which
aptitudes combine, relatively few indicate specific, well-
known occupations and professions.

The combination of any aptitude with extreme subjectivity
is awkward to study because of the infinite diversity among
subjective persons. Number memory, used in keeping stock,
in production planning or industrial scheduling, leads the
objective man through interim training grounds to executive
promotion. While equally suitable for anyone with number
memory, these same responsibilities leave the extremely subjective man at a blind end. He must find comparable activities,
worthwhile to himself, by transferring the studied application
from the business and industrial world to some profession
where this aptitude probably retains its inherent qualities.
Weather prediction, a division of meteorology, may fascinate
high number memory, which in another environment would
find outlet in stock market trading, with its price fluctuatiohs
and future predictions. The loving care of priceless editions
in a great library, while not called stock keeping, no doubt
requires the same number memory. The custodian of paintings, bronzes, jewels, for an art museum knows his possessions,
even when not on view, much as the good storekeeper knows
instantly the position of every article.

XI

THE DEXTERITIES

An extremely subjective carefully dressed man. at the ɪooth
percentile in accounting aptitude, ran a business machine for
six years in a brokerage house. Ten days before taking tests
he felt suddenly that he could stand his job no longer, left it,
and shifted to actual bench work involved in making hand-
wrought silver and arts-and-crafts jewelry. In finger dexterity he graded *A*, at the 85th percentile; in ideaphoria and
pitch discrimination he graded *B*, at the 65th percentile in
both, just below these in tonal memory, and unquestionably
low in structural visualization, which he will now need.

Clerical work and machine tabulating use accounting aptitude. In shifting to jewelry construction with his own hands the man used his second trait, finger dexterity, but lost the use of accounting aptitude. While the Laboratory has not yet been able to plan a research project which would evaluate statistically the insistence of using finger dexterity, numerous isolated instances suggest that this trait when idle leads as directly as any other to restlessness and dissatisfaction. The danger is this kind of transfer, from an occupation which uses a top 100th-percentile aptitude to one which uses a second but offers little hope of integrating the two.

Besides finger dexterity, jewelry construction probably uses pitch discrimination, once thought to apply specifically to musical performance, but which now seems to be a general niceness of sense perception, a characteristic of photographers as well as musicians. Where the artificer has freedom of design he uses ideaphoria. But this man held a self-achieved social position, and owned his own home, which demanded steady earnings. These he gave up when he started as a jewelry apprentice, with the hope of rising rapidly again. But with low structural visualization there seems little chance of his gaining the top as a recognized craftsman, and with an extremely subjective personality equally little chance of his developing a manufacturing organization. His aptitude pattern presents a challenge to which he has not yet found the solution.

XII

OBSERVATION

Observation as measured by worksample 206, forms CA and CB, grows to age eighteen or twenty with boys, figure 12, remains at this mature level for less than ten years, and begins at twenty-seven to drop steadily, so that men over forty-five average below boys of eleven. This may lead to the popular impression that children are more observant than their elders. With girls the same trait matures three years earlier, at fifteen or sixteen, remains at this adult level to the age of twenty-eight or twenty-nine, and then drops as with men.

The physical cause of this falling off with advancing age, shown to an exaggerated extent by observation, is as yet unexplained. If due to the hardening of the eye's focusing mechanism, which starts before thirty, worksample 380, a number-checking test paralleling worksample 268 but printed in large type, should reduce the drop and postpone its start. But virtually every aptitude shows this age drop slightly, though for each it begins at a different point. Unquestionably the self-conscious adult is less amenable to tests than the high-school pupil. He apologizes before he tries, gives up easily, and is reluctant to throw himself wholeheartedly into any performance. In the past, the research department has assumed that perfect administration should overcome the old age decline; but almost every test still shows it.

With the gradually strengthening evidence that each person possesses each aptitude in full or not at all has come a new point of view, the belief that this old age decline may be a natural lowering of aptitudes after forty which corresponds to growth before twenty. Although accepted without question as little is actually known about the growth mechanism as of the late shrinking.

Partly on the assumption that the age drop was spurious and should vanish with improved testing, partly because older men and women compete with younger persons and should be judged by the same standards, the research department has until now scored all examinees beyond maturity on adult plateau norms. This means that among older men and women, ages forty, forty-five, and fifty, more than half fall below the adult-plateau median. This conflicts with the present interpretation of the facts. On the adult plateau, and presumably at every age, one-half of men possess to the full such an aptitude as structural visualization, while the other half possess to an equal degree abstract visualization. This implies that the medians for the older ages must be lowered, so that at each point half of men score above and half below. The drop may still be eyesight, self-consciousness, or a general slowing of physical reactions, but until research shows otherwise the Laboratory will now score each age on its own norms, extending the practice previously applied to youth.

FIGURE 12

CHANGE OF OBSERVATION WITH AGE FOR MEN
WORKSAMPLE 206 FORM CA

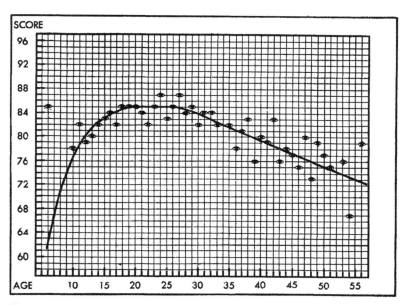

ACROSS THE BOTTOM THE FIGURES 10, 15, 20, TO 55 AT THE RIGHT ARE AGE
AT TIME OF TEST APPOINTMENT. EACH VERTICAL LINE REPRESENTING A
DIFFERENT AGE. THE VERTICAL SCALE AT THE LEFT INDICATES SCORE IN THE
TEST. EACH TINY SYMBOL SHOWS THE SEPARATELY DETERMINED MEDIAN
FOR EACH AGE. THE HEAVY LINE RISING FROM ABOUT 60 AT AGE 6, TO 85 AT
AGE 20, AND THEN DROPPING AGAIN AT AGE 26, SHOWS THE CHANGE OF
THE MEDIAN WITH AGE, AND THE SHORT ADULT PLATEAU FROM 20 TO 26.

Observation should be used; of this there seems abundant
proof. For the child who scores above the median, above the
heavy line drawn through the dots of figures 12 and 13, and
perhaps to an equal extent for the adult, the presence of a
balanced aquarium is one of countless observational exercises.
If this be surrounded by books on miniature fish and aquatic
plants, it is only a step from watching water life to looking
at pictures, and then to reading names, captions, and even the
text. The following books collected by Winifred Sorensen
surround the Laboratory's aquarium in Chicago:

FIGURE 13

CHANGE OF OBSERVATION WITH AGE FOR WOMEN
WORKSAMPLE 206 FORM CA

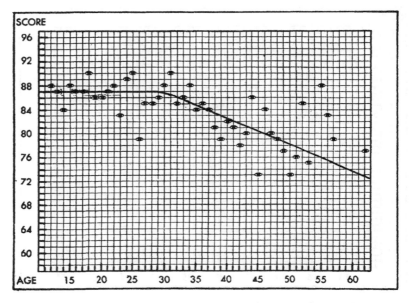

A COMPARISON OF THIS WITH FIGURE 12 SUGGESTS THAT OBSERVATION MATURES
EARLIER WITH WOMEN THAN WITH MEN, AND REMAINS ON THE ADULT PLATEAU
THREE YEARS LATER, NOT BEGINNING TO DROP BEFORE AGE 29.

FISHES by Bertha Morris Parker of the Laboratory Schools, University of Chicago, checked by Walter H. Chute, director of the John G. Shedd Aquarium, Chicago, Row, Peterson and Company, Evanston, Illinois, 1941. Price 35 cents. This inexpensive pamphlet, and the one which follows in this list, should be on the library shelves of every child high in observation or for any other reason interested in nature study.

TROPICAL FISH by Lucile Quarry Mann, revised edition 1943, A Sentinel Book, New York. Price 35 cents.

TROPICAL FISHES FOR THE HOME by Frederick H. Stoye, 1935, Sayville, New York.

EXOTIC AQUARIUM FISHES by William T. lnnes, 500 pp., natural color photographs, Innes Publishing Company.

TOADS AND FROGS by Bertha Morris Parker, Laboratory Schools, University of Chicago. Basic Science Educational Series, 1942, Row, Peterson and Company, Evanston, Illinois.

TROPICAL FISH HANDBOOK, 1944, published by Guenther L. Schott, New York.

AN AQUARIUM by Glenn O. Blough, 1943, Row, Peterson and Company, Evanston, Illinois.

THE MODERN AQUARIUM by William T. Innes, 1943, Philadelphia.

GOLDFISH VARIETIES by William T. Innes, Innes Publishing Company, Philadelphia.

HISTORY OF FISHES by J. R. Norman, published by Ernest Benn, Ltd., London, England.

A scientifically minded boy who scores high in observation should early be given a good microscope, not a toy, but a laboratory instrument. In addition he should own illustrated books showing microscopic photographs: the minute life of stagnant water, the crystalline structure of metallic alloys, sections of plant cells, living bacteria.

One high in observation should collect innumerable objects planned around his interests, living plants, animals which change and perpetually challenge his observation, caterpillars which can be watched through the cocoon and chrysalis to the mature butterfly, a beehive or ant's nest. Every boy high in observation should visit museums, not once but many times and regularly. Observation should be given every outlet.

XIII

THE FINE ARTS

Because three-quarters of mankind score OBJECTIVE in personality and belong in business, the public views the fine arts as appropriate only for the exception, a correct inference. For the extremely subjective minority they offer a natural life and frequently the greatest chance of happiness.

An extremely subjective man of thirty-three scored as shown in table L. With no significant responses on form AE of work-sample 35, and three on form FJ, he belongs in a profession, not in business. Because of his high abstract visualization and low structural visualization, he should handle ideas, not things. But the war caught him operating a turret lathe and he continued longer than on any previous job; for sixteen years, from the age of fourteen when he quit school at the end of

TABLE L

AROUND THE WORLD ON A TRAMP FREIGHTER

extremely subjective	in personality
high (90th percentile)	in abstract visualization
average (50th percentile)	in accounting aptitude
average (40th percentile)	in tonal memory
average (40th percentile)	in proportion appraisal
low (11th percentile)	in structural visualization
low (10th percentile)	in inductive reasoning
low	in other aptitudes
average (33d percentile)	in English vocabulary

FOR WANT OF FORMAL EDUCATION, NO MORE THAN EIGHTH GRADE, THIS MAN HAS NEVER MADE THE PROFESSIONAL PLACE SUITABLE TO HIS EXTREME SUBJECTIVITY AND ABSTRACT VISUALIZATION. INSTEAD HE HAS FAILED AT SELLING, BECAUSE OF LOW IDEAPHORIA; AND NOW WORKS UNHAPPILY AT A TURRET LATHE, WITH NO PROSPECTS BECAUSE OF HIS LOW STRUCTURAL VISUALIZATION.

eighth grade to thirty, he changed jobs annually. He had been around the world on tramp freighters, had seen most parts of the United States, and tried to sell. Clearly he had never found his niche. It was not turret lathe operation, for he scores too low in structural visualization to advance pleasurably in mechanical work; not selling, for he scores extremely subjective and low in ideaphoria. Clerical work leading to accounting would use accounting aptitude and extreme subjectivity; but his rambling travels reveal an aesthetic urge to use tonal memory and proportion appraisal. But he lacks the knowledge for self-expression. Extreme subjectivity demands an unconditional perfection greater than his present English vocabulary allows. Because extreme subjectivity prefers to build one subject at a time, he should study separately accounting, art, and music, seeking a common area.

XIV

PROPORTION APPRAISAL

In the sciences, the exact evaluation of each new factor means general and often spectacular progress, pushing research into regions which a few years earlier seemed impenetrable. Could some aesthetic factor be isolated, defined, and precisely measured, a new art vista might appear. Those who fear the restrictions which such a scientifically formulated aesthetic law would set up should read Clive Bell's dictum that great art appears only amid rigid limitations which stimulate effort.

After many false starts, proportion appraisal, as measured by worksample 235, now seems one such single element which enters the fine arts. The trait grows with age as do other aptitudes, reaching an early adult plateau, and thus differing from knowledge, as symbolized by English vocabulary, which improves through life.

Dr. Margaret McAdory made one of the first controlled attempts to measure art appreciation. Each item of her finished test depicts, in half-tone or occasionally in color, four slightly dissimilar objects, in one instance four library tables, labeled A, B, C, and D. She asks which the examinee prefers, entering the corresponding letter on a form which reads:

	1	2	etc.
Best	. . . . . .		
Next Best	. . . . . .		
Third Best	. . . . . .		
Worst	. . . . . .		

In another item Dr. McAdory shows four candlesticks, one a studied design and the others vitiated in three progressive steps. In a third item four rugs appear, in this instance in color.

Artists chose Dr. McAdory's selected answers with satisfactory uniformity; but the Laboratory's run of examinees also chose her answers with almost equal consistency. Only the rarest stroke of genius could change a design so skilfully as to be recognized by the gifted artist, but not by the world.

After a series of ineffective attempts to better the McAdory test through statistical analysis and selection of items, the Laboratory experimented with four museum objects, all of recognized quality, but nevertheless presumably differing in merit. One item portrayed pen and ink drawings of four Duncan Phyfe chairs, all designed by the same man, at approximately the same period. Here the Laboratory started with no preconceived opinion. As with the original McAdory test the concerted estimate of the Laboratory's examinees agreed with artists. The latter agree more consistently among themselves than do people in general; but the first choice of the masses is also the first choice of the artists. In this version individuals scattered more widely than formerly, only about one in four actually agreeing with artists. This meant greater accuracy of selection than before; but preliminary investigation showed the test too complex to warrant further analysis. The Laboratory then turned away from familiar objects to its present proportion-appraisal test, which shows in one item four rectangles of different proportions, in another four differing ovals, in another four triangles. Here the Laboratory clearly has no authority for deciding which proportion is right, which wrong. Instead, by actual administration of the proportion-appraisal test, worksample 235, it determined for each geometric shape the popular proportion. In determining the second most popular proportion, the research department has two options. Each person marks the four choices as: BEST, SECOND BEST, THIRD BEST, WORST. The first choice is clearly the one of the four marked BEST by the largest percentage of those who take the test. The second choice might be the one chosen as best by the next largest number, and originally the Laboratory chose this method.

Another method of determining the second choice is to pick that proportion marked as second best by the largest number. The two methods often agree; but when they differ, the last gives greater consistency of final choice. Similarly one can choose as WORST that marked BEST by the fewest people, or that marked WORST by the largest number, the latter again slightly preferable. The difference is never striking; one may call a design THIRD BEST which the other calls WORST.

The individual who today chooses a proportion as BEST which is marked BEST by a majority of people receives a score of one for this choice. The individual who marks as second best a proportion chosen as second best by a majority receives again one toward his final score. A total of four is the maximum for each plate and zero the minimum. With fifty plates, which is the number now used, the maximum score for the test as a whole is two hundred, and, allowing for the chance marking of the right answer, the minimum is fifty. One should remember exactly what the score means — agreement with popular opinion and perhaps nothing more. One who scores high agrees with the majority thus far tested; one who scores low disagrees.

From this, one can reason with some justification that a commercial artist, who must appeal to the masses, should score high, and the Laboratory often stresses this aspect of the test. Remember, however, as with each aptitude which the Laboratory measures, that this is only a single isolated factor in art success. As in every field, other traits are needed; and one who lacks proportion appraisal may achieve brilliant success through other traits or even by capitalizing on the lack of this one.

A satisfactory test often reveals some underlying consistency. One of the weaknesses of the McAdory Art Test, from which sprang the Laboratory's present proportion-appraisal test, was that among the popular choices there appeared no recognizable principle. This may, of course, have been the Laboratory's blindness; but the McAdory test proved too complex to react to statistical purification.

Items of the new proportion-appraisal test, worksample 235, which check with the final score are simple figures: rectangles, triangles, ovals, seen as relations of height to width, in contrast to frames, figures within figures, a square within a square. With simple figures the popular proportion is two by three, the least popular one by four in the original test, one by three in the revision. To avoid a set attitude and the habitual selection of the same proportion throughout, frames and complex figures, with different popular proportions, are interspersed between the single figures.

The early plateau of the age curve suggests that proportion appraisal is an inherent aptitude, as dynamic as structural visualization or ideaphoria, which should be used exactly as any other measurable trait. The agreement of popular opinion with the concerted judgment of artists may show an instinctive good taste of humanity as a whole. If so, the sequence of proportions for plane figures: two by three at the top, one by three and one by four at the bottom, may be a fundamental aesthetic law within which future artists should work.

But those on whom the study is based are of necessity alive at the time, successful during their lives, with no guarantee of future greatness. Prosperous artists may be those whose judgments chance to agree with the populace. If so, a high score in proportion appraisal, worksample 235, is a characteristic of contemporary artists.

Much as fashions change, so may scores in worksample 235. Redfield, in his book MUSIC, traces the world's appreciation of harmony. Once only the octave was a chord. Then the listening world admitted the triad, and heard the musical third, the octave simultaneously becoming too obvious for the sophisticated ear of that period. Then, a century later, the musical fifth ceased to be a discord. The fourth, and now the seventh, have in turn joined the accepted concords. Perhaps a proportion such as two by three, now thought pleasant, may, by slow, progressive steps, grow hackneyed a hundred years from now. This can be determined only by continued experimentation. The Laboratory knows as yet too little about the vocational significance of proportion appraisal to be of much practical assistance.

A sturdily built man of thirty-eight, table LII, married and with two children, earning $5000 a year by selling insurance, declared that he had reached the end of his tether; he would do anything to escape from selling, take evening courses, start at the beginning, but he could sell no longer; it suddenly nauseated him. Any man at the 100th percentile in ideaphoria, especially when reenforced by youthful energy and two additional sales traits, average accounting aptitude and low inductive reasoning, sells successfully so long as commissions mount annually. But one who scores extremely subjective rarely continues happily. He explained that he never sold on what he called PERSONALITY, made no effort to give his customers a good time, rarely bought them a drink, but presented established facts intellectually; and yet this extremely subjective man fought a constantly increasing dislike for sales work, and at the age of thirty-eight suddenly revolted.

TABLE LI

TRAITS COMMON TO COMMISSION SALESMEN

high	ideaphoria
objective	personality
average	accounting aptitude
low	structural visualization
low	inductive reasoning

FIVE INHERENT APTITUDES FOUND COMMONLY AMONG ALL TYPES OF SALESMEN.

Like others who turn against selling, he suggested its antithesis, engineering design. In this he would use his structural visualization and extreme subjectivity, as well as his ideaphoria. In acoustical engineering, in sound production and recording, he might use in addition his musical traits: tonal memory and pitch discrimination; and since this work is largely electrical and so highly mathematical, he might in addition tax his accounting aptitude. But with only a year of high-school physics, there seems no point in leaving sales for engineering. An objective man might chance the shift with the expectation of an executive place achieved through general background; but extreme subjectivity is uneasy without thorough grounding and rigid technical training.

Like so many salesmen who score high in structural visualization, this man's first thought was the selling of some technically designed device; but distributors of engineered products score like salesmen, table LI, objective in personality and low in structural visualization, not like engineers.

The man felt desperate enough to do anything and the temptation of the Laboratory staff was to concur with his own expressed willingness to start a three-year electrical engineering course. But in high school he had not done well in mathematics, for 100th-percentile ideaphoria rarely submits to rigid mathematical discipline. He had at one time enrolled in law school, but again, probably because of 100th-percentile ideaphoria, the professional restrictions irked him and he left. There seemed little chance of his persevering in engineering.

TABLE   LII

 APTITUDE SCORES OF AN INSURANCE SALESMAN

high (100th percentile)	in ideaphoria
high (95th percentile)	in tonal memory
high (85th percentile)	in accounting aptitude
high (80th percentile)	in pitch discrimination
extremely subjective	in personality
high (75th percentile)	in proportion appraisal
high (75th percentile)	in analytical reasoning
average to high (70th percentile)	in memory for design
average to high (62nd percentile)	in structural visualization
low (20th percentile)	in inductive reasoning

LIKE MANY WHO SCORE EXTREMELY SUBJECTIVE IN PERSONALITY, THIS MAN SOLD SUCCESSFULLY FOR A NUMBER OF YEARS AND THEN AT THE AGE OF THIRTY-EIGHT REBELLED AT SELLING. INDUSTRIAL ART DESIGN, IMPROVING THE APPEARANCE OF PACKAGES. WRAPPINGS, BOTTLES. AND CONTAINERS OF ALL TYPES, WOULD PROBABLY USE HIS TOTAL PATTERN.

Near the end of a discussion period, in which these facts came gradually to the surface, the man himself mentioned commercial package design; as a child he had studied art and enjoyed it. Commercial design would use his structural visualization not only in devising new shapes for ink bottles and electric irons, but in adapting them to economical machine production. It would use his sales experience, his proportion appraisal and memory for design, and give his ideaphoria unlimited scope; and top achievement in artistic packaging does not involve the long steady years of technical training required to mount in the engineering profession. He naturally thought first of products which have recognized the importance of design: silverware, furniture, clothing; but here, though he might contribute, he would compete with trained designers. The untrained man, especially with high ideaphoria and sales training, should direct his attention to some industry where the contribution of design is not yet accepted.

The mother of a shy, smiling girl, age twelve, table LIII, was told by the eighth grade·teacher that her daughter should not

TABLE LIII

A Twelve-Year-Old Girl

high (100th percentile)   ideaphoria
extremely subjective   personality
      (zero significant responses)
high (80th percentile)   proportion appraisal
low (15th percentile)   tonal memory
low (10th percentile)   accounting aptitude
very high   knowledge of birds
low (5th percentile)   English vocabulary

JUDGING BY APTITUDES SHE UNQUESTIONABLY BELONGS IN CREATIVE ART. THE MOTHER SUGGESTED SOME SORT OF ADVERTISING OR COMMERCIAL ART; BUT THIS IS NOT THE GOAL FOR SO SUBJECTIVE A CHILD. SHE SHOULD GAIN MORE BACKGROUND BY BROADENING HER KNOWLEDGE OF BIRDS TO A KNOWLEDGE OF FLOWERS AND THEN OF NATURAL HISTORY IN GENERAL.

take the college preparatory course in high school, reasonable advice, difficult to combat, for school marks reflect only the girl's two lowest traits. But the Laboratory believes it impossible to use 100th-percentile creative imagination without equivalent knowledge to accompany it and recommended preparation for a small, recently founded college offering art criticism and history and giving credit for original work, difficult advice to pursue, for every high-school course leading to college is hard for one low in both accounting aptitude and vocabulary, and at the end of every term this girl's school marks will reaffirm her unfitness for advanced education.

The father and mother, both previously tested, own a Vocabulary Builder and promised to start with the first word, HORSESHOER, and read aloud the discussions of two words a day. Ordinarily the Laboratory would entertain little hope of this girl's approximating in accomplishment her inherent capabilities, except that in the identification of birds, work-sample 353, she scored at a professional level. Her parents heard birds talked incessantly for a while after a bird walk, but regarded it as a passing childish fancy, with no idea that her knowledge ranked high by adult standards. Any child who can achieve so remarkable a knowledge in a short time can duplicate the feat in another field. Her parents should add bird books to her library; not ordinarily new recent expensive editions, but used copies, picked up second hand. With patience to wait and a willingness to buy any book one happens to find on one's own subject, even one financially limited can gather an exhaustive library. This child should enlarge her flower knowledge. and collect books on subjects allied to birds, perhaps trees, butterflies, insects.

THE ROAD OF A NATURALIST, 1941; GREEN LAURELS, 1936; FLOWERING EARTH, 1939; SINGING IN THE WILDERNESS, 1935; and AUDUBON'S AMERICA, 1940; all by Donald Culross Peattie, and published by Houghton Mifflin, might interest her.

SOCIAL LIFE AMONG THE INSECTS by William Morton Wheeler. Harcourt, Brace and Company. 1923; Professor Wheeler's titles suggest opportunities in this field: Professor of Economic Entomology; Dean of Bussey Institution; Research Associate, American Museum of Natural History.

SOCIAL LIFE IN THE INSECT WORLD by J. H. Fabre, translated by Bernard Miall, The Century Company, 1915.

THE SMITHSONIAN SCIENTIFIC SERIES, published in twelve volumes by the Smithsonian Institution in Washington. This set includes: Minerals, North American Indians, Insects, Wild Animals, Man from the Past, and Shelled Invertebrates.

The Laboratory has developed a knowledge-of-flowers test, worksample 355, comparable to the knowledge of birds, which this girl ought to take in a second appointment a year after her first; also a knowledge of animals. worksample 354, and a knowledge of paintings. This last aroused a flicker of interest when mentioned; but with an extremely subjective person it is hard to evaluate the strength of a budding enthusiasm.

For any child, or even adult, at the 100th percentile in ideaphoria, the effort to start at a 5th percentile general English vocabulary and build methodically is superhuman;

but a specialized knowledge already present, such as this child's knowledge of birds, can be strengthened, broadened, and combined with other types of knowledge, until the collection becomes a general background.

XV

MEMORY FOR DESIGN

A boy of eighteen, starting his last year in high school, scored extremely subjective in personality, and high in memory for design. Two or three weeks later his irate father appeared at the Laboratory. He did not understand the so-called bargraph, the graphical representation of scores given at the close of the test appointment, and, as he expressed it, had thrown away his thirty dollars. In addition the brochure, on which depends the interpretation, failed to discuss memory for design, the boy's top trait. Third, the test administrator mentioned cartooning, which seemed to the father childishly impractical. All three criticisms were justified, as were others which he had not formulated so sententiously. After twenty years of experimentation the Laboratory does not yet know how to present its results intelligibly and, with additional research findings, the task becomes no easier. The seventeen or eighteen now measurable separate aptitudes combine in several hundred thousand different ways. The Laboratory does not pretend to understand all of these combinations or even a large fraction. Only some four hundred, less than one per cent, fit perfectly known jobs with recognized names. The Laboratory has no proved, practical suggestion for the extremely subjective boy with memory for design as his top trait. Fitting together bits of data, memory for design seems to be a gift for carrying in mind pictures of things seen. Compared with a portrait painter who copies his sitter, or a landscape painter who works from an easel before his scene, a cartoonist draws on his mind for the pose of a political candidate, a galloping horse. a city sky line, or a circus lion. A mural painter and an illustrator do the same perhaps to a lesser extent. All such creative art is subjective. Cartooning is perhaps the best illustration of high memory for design with subjectivity. But no boy should enter cartooning because of these two traits, or for any other combination of aptitudes. In this case the boy scored low in ideaphoria, undoubtedly needed in cartooning. On the other hand, with five more years of education ahead, if he finishes college, the Laboratory believes that one course should be taken in pen and ink sketching or in free-hand charcoal drawing, if not during the school term then during a summer. In many fields facility with a pencil adds to success, and always gives pleasure.

Second, the boy scored low in accounting aptitude and belonged in just such a small preparatory school as he was attending. He also belonged in a small college instead of the huge midwestern university in which he was already enrolled. Because of low vocabulary the boy belonged in a recently founded college such as the father had already picked.

Prior to the appointment, with no test scores to guide him, the father had chosen a recently founded midwestern college, in the belief that it was less academic and so more suitable to a boy already a year retarded, who had never found school work easy, than an older eastern school. Sensing that the boy belonged in a profession, and was temperamentally unsuited to the business world, the father had chosen a general college, but one offering technical engineering courses which the boy might elect if he found them congenial.

What could the Laboratory contribute to a father who had considered so carefully a son's requirements? Based on the boy's low vocabulary, it agreed with the selection of a recently founded non-academic college, but because of low accounting aptitude it preferred a small college. This point seemed sufficiently important so that the test administrator selected, and presented at the close of the appointment, a brochure which discussed selection of college, rather than one which included memory for design.

Because the boy scored extremely subjective in personality, the Laboratory agreed with the father that he should be given professional training, and not plan on business; but the boy scored low in structural visualization and the Laboratory felt that the opportunities offered the boy during college should be non-structural, and if possible challenging to memory for design, rather than engineering in nature. By a study of the college statistics tabulated at the back of STRUCTURAL VISUALIZATION the father later found a college which suited perfectly his own requirements as well as those of the Laboratory.

TABLE LIV

APTITUDE SCORES OF A SEVENTEEN-YEAR-OLD GIRL
A HIGH-SCHOOL SENIOR

extremely subjective	personality
high (95th percentile)	memory for design
average (60th percentile)	accounting aptitude
average (60th percentile)	tweezer dexterity
average (58th percentile)	structural visualization
average (55th percentile)	ideaphoria
average (55th percentile)	finger dexterity
average (50th percentile)	observation
average (40th percentile)	tonal memory
low (15th percentile)	inductive reasoning
low (10th percentile)	proportion appraisal

FOR AERONAUTICAL ENGINEERING THIS GIRL SHOULD SCORE ABOVE THE 75TH PERCENTILE IN STRUCTURAL VISUALIZATION. IN PRIVATE DUTY NURSING, WHICH SHE SUGGESTED, SHE WOULD USE ACCOUNTING APTITUDE, TWEEZER DEXTERITY, AND HER EXTREME SUBJECTIVITY. OCCUPATIONAL THERAPY WAS THE FINAL SUGGESTION AS LIKELY TO SATISFY HER DESIRE TO HELP OTHERS, WHICH DREW HER TOWARD NURSING, TO USE HER MEMORY FOR DESIGN IN THE ART WHICH CAN BE MADE AN IMPORTANT PART OF OCCUPATIONAL THERAPY; AND TO USE HER TWEEZER DEXTERITY, STRUCTURAL VISUALIZATION, IDEAPHORIA, AND FINGER DEXTERITY, IN THE HANDWORK OF OCCUPATIONAL THERAPY.

A girl of seventeen, table LIV, a high-school senior, with a single significant response on forms AE and FJ combined, thought vaguely of aeronautical engineering, largely because of a brother in the air force. With the engineer's personality, ideaphoria above the median, and structural visualization not far below the critical 75th-percentile for women, the Laboratory would hesitate to advise against engineering with one keenly interested; but this girl knew that her desire would not withstand repeated discouragements.

She spoke next of nursing. This requires high accounting aptitude and high tweezer dexterity, but would not challenge this girl's memory for design nor her wide range of aptitudes. Cartooning would use her top two traits, high memory for design and extreme subjectivity, but seemed too far removed from her interests to stress solely on aptitudes. Like nursing, occupational therapy is closely associated with the medical profession, remedial in aim, and likely to give function to a range of aptitudes. For those at the top occupational therapy is a profession and so suitable for one who scores extremely subjective. It does not demand specifically high accounting aptitude. Because the occupational therapist may turn her interest toward any craft it offers challenge to many aptitudes. without demanding any one to the exclusion of others. It would give this girl a chance to use structural visualization if she possesses it and to try cartooning without risking her whole future on so doubtful an occupation.

XVI

ENGLISH VOCABULARY

At some critical age near forty the business world shifts its tacit judgment from a sanguine consideration of inherent aptitudes and their future promise to a detached appraisal of finished accomplishments indicated by acquired English vocabulary. The youthful graduate of a large midwestern state college, after working earnestly four years, returned to business school, and then joined the advertising department of a national organization merchandizing dairy products. He rose to assistant advertising head, when a financial merger with a rival concern wafted him to an ideal position as product supervisor attached to the sales department. Subsequently, when tested, he scored as shown in table LV.

Salesmanship is always creative; planning on a national scale needs inductive reasoning. The practical development of novel products gives some vent to structural visualization. The work did not force constant contact with the public, but rather an intellectual analysis congenial to the subjective temperament.

It also embraced sufficient statistical discussion of distribution records to satisfy his accounting aptitude; and he rose to an annual salary of twelve thousand dollars as assistant to the sales promotion manager. Then a second upheaval stranded him in an organization eddy which he regarded as inferior

.   TABLE LV

PRODUCT SUPERVISOR

very high, grade $A+$	in tonal memory
very high, grade $A+$	in inductive reasoning
high, grade A	in ideaphoria
high, grade A	in observation
high, grade A	in structural visualization
high, grade $B+$	in accounting aptitude
extremely subjective	in personality
average (51st percentile)	in vocabulary

AS ASSISTANT TO THE SALES PROMOTION MANAGER THIS MAN ROSE TO A LARGE SALARY IN WORK WHICH USED ALMOST EVERY APTITUDE HE POSSESSED. INDUCTIVE REASONING HE USED IN PLANNING NATIONAL SALES CAMPAIGNS; IDEAPHORIA BOTH IN NOVEL SALES IDEAS AND IN CREATING NEW PRODUCTS. STRUCTURAL VISUALIZATION HE USED IN INTRODUCING NEW PRODUCTS INTO THE FACTORY. OBSERVATION HE USED IN A CONSTANT SUPERVISION OF QUALITY; ACCOUNTING APTITUDE IN HIS STATISTICAL ANALYSES OF SALES RECORDS. BUT AT THE AGE OF FORTY HE WAS DEMOTED, THE LABORATORY BELIEVES BECAUSE HE HAD RISEN TO A POSITION ABOVE HIS 51ST PERCENTILE VOCABULARY, NEGLECTING TO KEEP HIS KNOWLEDGE IN PACE WITH HIS ADVANCEMENT.

and which certainly used neither ideaphoria nor structural visualization and which required an objective rather than extremely subjective personality.

At this point he came to the Human Engineering Laboratory with the solemn query: Should he seek a new employer and if so of what type; or was he merely emotionally wrought up by forced readjustments? Any man with five grade A aptitudes is restless; many are the proverbial jack-of-all-trades, good at none. Even in the job which this man most enjoyed, in which he reached his earning peak, he had not exercised his tonal memory, except in musical enjoyment, a satisfactory solution only if integrated finally into life's goal. The planning of sales campaigns for radio broadcasting might have been a forward step; but the complete unification of such an aptitude array calls for a unique solution, not work universally known by a stereotyped name.

The agricultural development of South America attracted him, an undertaking weighty enough to tax any aptitude, and closely related to his handling of dairy products; but he persisted in regarding his daily work as a proscribed job, due in part to his mediocre knowledge of words, for the first step toward understanding any unsolved problem is a clear, concise statement of the issue.

Before visiting the Laboratory, the man felt certain of a large vocabulary; his wife mentioned it repeatedly; both thought his score unfair. The Laboratory struggles constantly to attract low-vocabulary examinees, for they need the encouraging incentive of knowing their inherent aptitudes; but that portion of the public which hears of human engineering is apt to have more than average knowledge, and in consequence scoring standards, which depend on a comparison with other people, are unintentionally severe. Compared with the whole of humanity this man undoubtedly scores high, but higher still in at least five aptitudes, for in both tonal memory and inductive reasoning he rates above the 95th percentile based on the same tested population. Approaching forty, where the world calls for accomplished exploits, this man could not hope to hold much longer a position gained earlier through inherent potentialities. Transfer to an inferior job, in this case ostensibly as the result of company reorganization, comes to almost every low-vocabulary man.

With the same determination which this dairy-products sales executive puts into his work, he has undertaken to raise his fund of words from its present 51st percentile to the level of his top two aptitudes, where he will meet no further trouble; and research shows that he can advance, but no more quickly than earlier. During the customary school period, years of study are accepted as natural and essential to top achievement; but the adult who spends a major part of his energies in the day's work and who lacks the external stimulation which the authoritative teacher gives the child, anticipates phenomenal progress and feels that for him a few months should suffice.

One who starts education late in life must carry out exactly the same extended program which would lead the child to success, must face honestly the same number of years, the same hours per day, and the same financial cost of education. Stampeded by financial pressure, unpaid bills, and advancing age, adults suddenly discover that twelve years have actually gone while they are still where they were earlier. No matter what his age the adult must set his goal and then take one step at a time untroubled by the multitude which follow to carry him even a short distance; in vocabulary building, learn one or two words each day. He will not be great in a week, nor earn a large salary, but at the end of a dozen years will not have stood idle.

One hears the Laboratory misquoted as calling a large English vocabulary an executive feature. Exact knowledge character-izes successful men and women in all walks. OCCUPATIONAL Bookkeepers and accountants score alike in VOCABULARY basic aptitudes, but differ in knowledge, ac-LEVELS countants scoring 179 on the general vocabu-lary scale compared with bookkeepers at 143. In the structural occupations, mechanics, machinists, draftsmen, engineers, and scientists, score inherently remarkably alike; but machinists rank above mechanics in rate of pay, steadiness of working hours, and job security, and score significantly higher in vocabulary; while designing engineers, who enjoy still more privileges, score still higher.

At the top of this vocabulary ladder are the eminent men and women of the world, not only executives but editors, lawyers, engineers, and accountants; and those who gain this vocabulary peak are not always those who found it easiest. Most Americans realize the irreparable damage to the country should it lose these rare, high-vocabulary individuals; but, though less directly felt, the loss would be equally great should these same men have failed to lift themselves to their present levels.

A comparison of two hardware salesmen, tested by chance in the same week, one high and the other low in English vocabulary, shows how an exact and extensive knowledge of words helps in facing unforeseen exigencies. At the age of forty-one Mr. Low-Vocabulary submitted to defeat in the guise of a minor clerical job, blaming his inability to fill orders on the world war. High-Vocabulary crossed the Atlantic as a commissioned representative of the United States government, routing metal products to European allies.

TABLE LVI

An Actor who Tried to Sell

high (100th percentile)	accounting aptitude
high (100th percentile)	tonal memory
high (95th percentile)	abstract visualization
high (90th percentile)	pitch discrimination
extremely subjective	personality
(13 significant responses on forms AE and FJ)	
high (85th percentile)	proportion appraisal
high (80th percentile)	observation
average (50th percentile)	ideaphoria
low (20th percentile)	inductive reasoning
low (20th percentile)	analytical reasoning
low (20th percentile)	English vocabulary
low (6th percentile)	structural visualization

ACCOUNTING AS A PROFESSION WOULD USE THIS MAN'S HIGH ACCOUNTING APTITUDE AND EXTREME SUBJECTIVITY, BUT WOULD NEVER USE HIS HIGH TONAL MEMORY. SELLING, WHICH HE TRIED FOR EIGHT YEARS, USES SOME ACCOUNTING APTITUDE, ABSTRACT VISUALIZATION, IDEAPHORIA, AND LOW INDUCTIVE REASONING; BUT CONTINUED SELLING IS CONGENIAL ONLY TO THE OBJECTIVE TEMPERAMENT. THIS MAN BELONGS IN MUSICAL PERFORMING, AND WAS AT THE TOP OF THE NEW YORK MUSICAL THEATER WORLD WHEN, AT THE AGE OF THIRTY-SEVEN, HE DECIDED THAT IT OFFERED NO FUTURE. INABILITY TO SEE AN INSPIRING FUTURE SEEMS TO MARK THOSE WHOSE VOCABULARY IS BELOW THE LEVEL OF THE SUCCESS THEY HAVE ALREADY GAINED.

Women as well as men seek strange excuses for unfavorable happenings which regularly accompany low vocabularies in middle life. After ten years of lucrative dress design a woman of thirty-three complained that her business superiors, previously interested in her at twenty-five, no longer needed her analysis of fashion trends, of public demands, of future requirements. She prided herself on an analytical mind but felt that men disliked the trait in a woman associate. Should she stop analyzing? Should she instead talk down to her executives, a favorite idea with low-vocabulary examinees. Eight years earlier her employers saw promise in this woman's aptitude pattern; at thirty-three they judge her by what she

TABLE LVII

COMPARISON OF ACCOUNTING, ACTING, SELLING

	ACCOUNTING	THEATER	SELLING
accounting aptitude	challenged	idle	used
tonal memory	idle	challenged	idle
abstract visualization	used	used	used
pitch discrimination	idle	challenged	idle
extreme subjectivity	used	used	wrong
proportion appraisal	idle	challenged	idle
observation	idle	used	idle
ideaphoria	not needed	needed	needed

is, by her English vocabulary, where she scores at the 30th percentile, compared with major executives, who average at the 93d percentile. With her English vocabulary where it is, this woman cannot deal with superiors at their own high level, nor can she analyze intricate situations with verbal clarity. Any executive prefers a man or woman under twenty-five with a chance of developing, to one ten years older, with identical aptitudes and still a low vocabulary; for growing aptitudes stimulate the worker, but after these mature, from the age of twenty on, progress comes from increased skill and greater knowledge, one who scores the same in vocabulary at thirty-three as earlier turning out much the same sort of designs as earlier.

In certified public accounting, always a first thought with 100th-percentile accounting aptitude and extreme subjectivity, an interesting man of forty-five, whose aptitude pattern appears in table LVI, would use these two traits and the complementary pair, high abstract visualization and low structural visualization. But accountants score not so high as this man in the musical traits and higher in analytical reasoning.

Starting the interpretation again with his 100th-percentile tonal memory, high pitch discrimination, and extreme subjectivity, he belongs in music. This uses the same complementary pair, abstract visualization and low structural visualization, as well as ideaphoria. Some combination of art and music, of sight and sound, would use his proportion appraisal and observation as well.

For fifteen years this tall, thin aristocrat performed near the top of the New York theatrical musical world. Then he left the stage to sell. This used:

high	ideaphoria
high	abstract visualization
average	accounting aptitude
low	structural visualization
low	inductive reasoning

His only serious departure from the sales pattern was extreme subjectivity, contrasting with the objectivity of the perfect salesman. For eight years he succeeded in selling, and then came to be tested with the statement that he did not understand himself, felt somehow that he was wasting his life but had no idea what to do. In tabular form, table LVII, three fields challenge him to different degrees. After rising musically in the theater world, exactly where he belonged, this man left the stage at just the time of life when a low vocabulary, one below one's aptitudes, begins to hold one back. Many low-vocabulary men and women turn similarly from a field where they belong to another less suitable, unmindful that lack of knowledge, not lack of ability, limits further progress.

Without some sort of measured analysis a man frequently misinterprets his failure, altering his course to a worse direction. When advised by his employer to leave selling, because he lacked the essential vitality, a man who sold government bonds showed in terms of aptitudes, table LVIII, four of the ideal five sales traits: objectivity, ideaphoria, abstract visualization, and accounting aptitude at the 30th percentile, his only departure from the perfect pattern a high score in inductive reasoning. The organization for which he worked sold large blocks to insurance companies and small-town banks. With prices rigidly fixed, he offered a highly intangible service possible to describe only in words which he lacked. To aggravate his troubles he dealt directly with a high-vocabulary president, or other top executive, who gained nothing from

TABLE LVIII

A Bond Salesman

high (92nd percentile)	inductive reasoning
high (85th percentile)	ideaphoria
extremely objective	personality
(28 significant responses on form AE)	
high (80th percentile)	proportion appraisal
average (35th percentile)	analytical reasoning
low (30th percentile)	accounting aptitude
low (15th percentile)	observation
low (10th percentile)	tonal memory
low (5th percentile)	structural visualization
low (5th percentile)	pitch discrimination
low (5th percentile)	English vocabulary

WITH PRACTICALLY EVERY SALES APTITUDE, A RARE PATTERN, THIS MAN FAILED IN SELLING LARGE BLOCKS OF BONDS TO BANKS AND INSURANCE COMPANIES BECAUSE HIS LOW, 5TH-PERCENTILE, VOCABULARY MADE IT IMPOSSIBLE FOR HIM TO COMMUNICATE IDEAS TO TOP EXECUTIVES.

a salesman at the 5th percentile. He came to be tested convinced that he was no salesman and ready to accept minor clerical work with one of his customer banks, where accounting aptitude at the 30th percentile and ideaphoria at the 85th foretold almost certain failure. He failed in selling because of low vocabulary, not for lack of suitable aptitudes. He should continue in the general sales direction, though high inductive reasoning suggests advertising rather than straight selling. Until he materially lifts his knowledge of English words, he should sell to prospective buyers at a lower vocabulary level than bank presidents and top insurance executives.

Far too often a man in exactly the right calling, needing only to continue adding to his knowledge, integrating his born gifts with his accumulating information and experience, feels himself a failure. Discharged from the army because of what he termed a mental condition, a tall, tense, aesthetic man of thirty obtained after repeated struggles an accounting position, and in a few months left it voluntarily with the plea that he was not doing so well as he should, the same apologetic reason which he gave for not returning to his former employers, a well-known public-accounting firm. After another troublesome interlude, he started once more and no sooner advanced to auditing than he imagined himself again inadequate.

The accounting-aptitude test, worksample 268, he finished in the incredibly short time of 3.06 minutes for five forms. At the 100th-percentile in figure 5, where seventy per cent of adult men take longer than 4.75 minutes, eighty per cent take longer than 4.50, and ninety-one per cent take longer than 4.00 minutes. On learning that he ranked above the recorded scoring scale, and yet feeling that he was not fast enough, he analyzed his own discontent with the remark: "I do not know enough". After thirty no man should change his work because of his aptitude pattern, unless his knowledge, expressed in percentiles, is as great as the aptitudes by means of which he gained his present place.

For anyone in a suitable field as the outcome either of intelligent planning or mere propinquity, accumulation of knowledge can be a delightful enterprise, but is easily postponed indefinitely and sometimes never seriously undertaken. Kept from his college plans by the death of his father, a seventeen-year-old boy did what he called the easiest thing, took up accounting with an insurance company to support his mother. Fourteen years later, at the age of thirty-one, he had grown to hate the monotony, and expected when tested to learn that he had never belonged in accounting. He sought some brand-new direction, but scored:

	high	in accounting aptitude,
	extremely subjective	in personality,
	low	in structural visualization,
and	low	in creative imagination,

exactly the accounting pattern. Why then should he dislike the work? He has every aptitude needed for the top, but not enough vocabulary, for on the general vocabulary scale he scores 169, not low, but ten points below the average accountant at 179, low enough to keep him from rising above the routine

TABLE LIX

A Licensed Electrician

extremely subjective	in personality
high	in tonal memory
high	in pitch discrimination
high	in observation
high	in proportion appraisal
low	in structural visualization
low	in accounting aptitude
low	in English vocabulary

COULD THIS MAN HAVE BEEN TESTED AS A CHILD THE LABORATORY WOULD HAVE URGED SOMETHING IN PROFESSIONAL MUSIC; BUT AT THIRTY-FOUR THIS IS USUALLY IMPRACTICAL. THE SAME APTITUDE PATTERN SUGGESTS PHOTOGRAPHY, WHICH IS POSSIBLE TO START AS AN AMATEUR.

of the profession. The only honest advice, though unwelcome, is to go on as an accountant and increase vocabulary.

Infinitely more pathetic than a man without knowledge of his own subject is one in wrong work who lacks the knowledge needed to use his aptitudes elsewhere. After a vocational course in electric wiring a nervously energetic little man practiced happily for 'eight years as a licensed electrician. Then he sought navy yard war work; but so chafed under both the rigid hours and what he considered the tyranny of an overbearing boss that he soon shifted to another navy yard, where he was equally unhappy. At this point he studied radio and became a research technician in an experimental laboratory. But his own two and a half years of formal high school were not enough to advance among college graduates; and furthermore he complained that many with doctor's degrees earned pitiful stipends. At the age of thirty-four he came to the Laboratory insisting that it tell him exactly what to do. He scored as shown in table LIX, a syndrome of aptitudes which indicate potential brilliance in a synthesis of art and music. Low structural visualization points away from science and engineering; low accounting aptitude away from clerical work and the run of desk jobs; and the combination of low accounting aptitude and extreme subjectivity diametrically away from commission selling which attracted him by its promise of the independence which he craved. Men in distasteful work, who must nevertheless continue to support themselves and their families, turn impulsively to illogical escapes against which they would counsel others. If the Laboratory did nothing but dissuade this man from commission selling it would have done its job.

Though a remote and ostensibly impractical goal he must use tonal memory, pitch discrimination, and proportion appraisal, as nuclei for further reading and fuller personal expression. Although at the time he was tested the Laboratory had no such notion, it now knows that this man's aptitude pattern fits commercial photography, which might have been a practical solution, for with his unbounded energy he could have started in spare time as a hobby, and judged by aptitudes risen high. Because persistent research discloses just such undreamt possibilities the Laboratory sends from time to time, to all who have been tested, reports of progress and urges the purchase of recent brochures.

Tested younger, perhaps at age nine, he might have placed himself in the fine arts; but at thirty-four, married and with two children, no new direction offered an immediate living to compete with electrical wiring. Some sort of compromise seemed the only practical solution; but his extreme subjectivity allowed him to accept nothing short of perfection. Because the subjective person is happiest in a field which he knows, the Laboratory wanted him to return to electrical wiring, where he had proved his ability to earn an adequate living, and meanwhile to work on his vocabulary and buy books on music and art. Though limited by financial obligations, this man must take vocabulary building seriously as the soundest approach to a satisfactory life for the extremely subjective person. He bought the Vocabulary Builder, but clearly felt the advice inadequate.

A mature man comes with responsibilities and cannot shift suddenly; but in actual life, during the past twenty years, the Laboratory has seen numerous extremely subjective men and women, highly dissatisfied with the outcome of the test appointment, nevertheless improve their vocabularies and

TABLE LX

APTITUDES WHICH SUGGEST LAW, WRITING, OR
COLLEGE TEACHING

extremely subjective	in personality
high	in abstract visualization
average (60th percentile)	in inductive reasoning
average (60th percentile)	in ideaphoria
low	in structural visualization

BECAUSE OF UNQUESTIONABLY LOW STRUCTURAL VISUALIZATION THIS MAN DOES NOT BELONG IN MECHANICAL WORK; BUT CIRCUMSTANCES FORCED HIM TO BECOME A SCREW-MACHINE OPERATOR. AFTER STAYING AWAY FROM HIS WORK FOR TWO WEEKS HE CAME TO BE TESTED. THOUGH NOT A COLLEGE GRADUATE, THE LABORATORY BELIEVES THAT HE SHOULD SPEND HIS SATURDAYS, SUNDAYS, AND EVENINGS IN TRYING TO WRITE.

ultimately rise to unique positions which formerly seemed chimerical, and which no administrator could foresee.

A heavily built man in his middle thirties belongs in a profession dealing with ideas, and the test administrator used law, writing, and college teaching, as illustrations. He replied testily that if law was the recommendation there was little point in his continuing with aptitude tests, for he had no college degree, only a year and a half of high school. Married, and with three children to support, he could not possibly return to four years of college. He scored as shown in table LX, with a perfect writing pattern. But few mortals, even when perfectly equipped, can earn a living wage by their pen alone. Gradually it transpired that he had undergone two nervous breakdowns, one several years earlier when he was doing mechanical work in industry, one while a mechanic in the army and for which he was discharged. For the previous two weeks, before taking tests, he had not been to work, unable to face the automatic screw machine which he operated.

Men low in an aptitude turn violently against work which demands it when too long and persistently continued under pressure. Although at first impatient with every suggestion, this man ultimately volunteered unprompted the advisability of his returning to his machine, earning the adequate living

TABLE LXI

APTITUDES WHICH SUGGEST ART

very high (95th percentile)	ideaphoria
high (95th percentile)	rhythm memory
high (90th percentile)	tweezer dexterity
extremely subjective	personality
high (80th percentile)	proportion appraisal
average (60th percentile)	tonal memory
low (20th percentile)	inductive reasoning
low (20th percentile)	accounting aptitude
low (5th percentile)	English vocabulary

IN FOLLOWING HIS FATHER IN SPECULATIVE BUILDING THIS BOY WOULD USE IDEAPHORIA IN BOTH DESIGN AND SELLING, TWEEZER DEXTERITY IN SUCH DRAFTING AS HE MIGHT DO, PROPORTION APPRAISAL IN THE MECHANICS OF BUILDING, AND LOW INDUCTIVE REASONING IN SELLING. THE ONLY FEAR IS THAT EXTREME SUBJECTIVITY RARELY FINDS CONTINUED HAPPINESS IN SALES PROMOTION. THE BOY MENTIONED LAW AND BANKING, THE LAST THE WORST DIRECTION HE COULD CHOOSE, FOR BANKING TAKES ACCOUNTING APTITUDE, OBJECTIVITY IN THE EXECUTIVE POSITIONS, AND NO IDEAPHORIA.

which it supplied, and meanwhile writing, his hidden ambition. He thought that knowing he lacked the mechanical gift would somehow make the perpetual oil of his machine easier to face; and if in addition he could devote four hours each Saturday and Sunday to writing it should increasingly ease the situation.

After twelve years in a cramped motion-picture projection booth, hung on the rear wall of a huge Philadelphia theater, an extremely subjective man of forty-five craved revolutionary advice; but he scored at the 5th percentile in vocabulary, and no field promises happiness to extreme subjectivity with this scant knowledge. An iconoclastic change of occupation might bestow fleeting satisfaction, but he would meet again the same need; and the quicker he faced honestly this gap the greater would be his chance of bridging it. Furthermore, the theater offers the extremely subjective person a stimulating life. To be sent back to one's same old prosaic job, after picturing an undreamt-of course, is uninspiring and clearly not always the solution, but is sometimes a practical expedient. Pathetically disillusioned by the outcome, suffering in his stifling surroundings, the man invested in aptitude tests to throw off the fetters of a life time; but he engaged ruefully to buy three second-hand books on stagecraft in as many months and to report back. He kept his promise, and during the period was visited in his booth by a playwright who heard of the man's desire for theater knowledge and, in the midst of a busy life, remembered once a month to send directly to the projection balcony a book from his own library. It transformed smothering confinement into a reception room with world contacts. Although the sequence of steps is seldom foreseen, the man who improves his vocabulary somehow finds expanding opportunity to use additional aptitudes.

In another case a man who had placidly routed freight cars for four and a half years scored:

extremely subjective	in personality,
high	in inductive reasoning,
high	in tweezer dexterity,
low	in number memory,
low	in structural visualization,
and low	in English vocabulary.

Scheduling of all types, also called routing, demands high number memory, and this man's deficiency substantiated his discontent. As an alternative he mentioned drafting, for facile tweezer dexterity frequently entices its possessor toward the clever manipulation of drawing instruments; but advancement from tracing to design demands structural visualization and here another lack would soon set up a new barrier. Length of service guaranteed a regular salary he could not duplicate elsewhere as a tyro. Though a man detests his present predicament, switch to agreeable work requires preparation; in this case high inductive reasoning demands exact words as tools.

Entering the Human Engineering Laboratory to discover hidden aptitudes, many persons feel imposed upon when the administrator neglects the live issue around which modern interest centers and urges instead old-fashioned, English vocabulary building. But scanty knowledge retards the average man or woman more often than meager ability. When the Laboratory minimizes aptitudes, it does not forget their existence, but believes that with that particular examinee they are not the limiting factor; for the Laboratory's aim goes beyond the measurement of aptitudes, to a broader understanding of human behavior.

In line with its policy as a research organization, the Human Engineering Laboratory states facts, rarely gives advice, and cannot squander undue time in the persuasion of one mortal. To help the fifteen thousand persons tested annually it must strive to make the entire world vocabulary conscious. But occasionally an examinee takes the attitude that a test administrator should convince him or her as an individual of the need to study. An attractive, impetuous girl of nineteen, remarkably high in aptitudes:

ACCEPTING ADVICE

above the 95th percentile	in ideaphoria,
above the 90th percentile	in analytical reasoning,
equally high	in observation,

with the social background which money gives, scored normal, at the 50th percentile, in vocabulary; and when the administrator urged more exact words she replied flatly that she saw no need for more than she possessed. She excelled in the primary grades, did less well in high school, and after a year of college decided she needed no more education, and left. The international opportunities of journalism attracted her; and the Laboratory had just measured a well-known group of editorial writers who showed exactly her traits, turning their high observation to war reporting, their ideaphoria and analytical reasoning to editorial comments; but they scored at the 96th percentile in vocabulary, compared with her 50th percentile. Through an acquaintance she obtained an assignment, but did not survive. As a born toolmaker, with no tools of his trade, competes but sadly with a perfectly equipped machine shop, so for effective use each inherent aptitude depends on corresponding knowledge, specifically on words, the essential tools of modern civilization. Perhaps because of this odd phenomenon the low-vocabulary boy turns instinctively from his top aptitudes to his weaker ones where the gap between low ability and little knowledge is easier to bridge.

An extremely subjective high-school junior, with two significant responses on the combined forms AE and FJ, scored as shown in table LXI. Ideaphoria, tweezer dexterity, proportion appraisal, and extreme subjectivity, are a perfect pattern for creative art, for which the boy showed no knowledge and perhaps in consequence no interest. His rhythm memory and tonal memory are high enough to suggest music, which the boy vaguely enjoyed but not enough to make it a life's work. His father sold real estate and made money in speculative building. This uses:

high	ideaphoria,
objective	personality, and
low	inductive reasoning,

the primary sales traits, with perhaps:

| high | structural visualization |

of the architect, although salesmen as a whole score low in structural visualization and high in abstract visualization.

In following his father the boy would use many of his own traits: certainly his high ideaphoria in selling; his tweezer dexterity in drafting if he did some of his own designing; and his proportion appraisal in the same way; but the statistical chances are against an extremely subjective boy ever finding real happiness in selling, his aptitudes clearly indicating something in the fine arts.

The boy's expressed interests are law and banking, the first dependent primarily on inductive reasoning, the second on accounting aptitude, the boy's two lowest traits. Frequently enough to be significant, the low-vocabulary examinee thus voices an interest in using his weakest aptitudes.

Aptitude studies fail thus far to substantiate the prevalent belief that age slows learning; but practical barriers certainly interfere. A twenty-year-old boy, still in sophomore year of high school, outside the normal age range centering around fifteen, scored low English vocabulary, low accounting aptitude, and left eyed in worksample 236, although he used his right hand. Low vocabulary retards two years in school; low accounting aptitude, when ignored, adds another two years, and the complication of the left eye and right hand suffices to explain this boy's five-year lag. Should he start at twenty, or give up, with the danger of becoming a public liability? Low accounting aptitude shows in test measurements as early as age nine. The boy should then have entered a small private school. with less than seventy pupils, for money was never a hindrance; instead he attended a large public school of a thousand or more. At age twenty the problem grows formidable; few schools want such a boy with others five years younger. At age nine he should have experimented with his left hand. At twenty he performs the tweezer-dexterity test, worksample 18, faster with his left than with his right, after declaring in advance he could do nothing with his left. Had the boy started conscious vocabulary building at age nine he might have graduated normally from college at twenty-one.

A father and mother, both college graduates who knew intimately the aims of the Human Engineering Laboratory from its inception, postponed the testing of their son for ten years, until as a high-school junior he scored five years retarded in vocabulary. Could this otherwise gifted boy have been measured at age nine he might have seen the need of words, and perhaps reached high school with normal understanding. Why these delightful parents, with sound academic backgrounds, should raise a low-vocabulary son, in the midst of cultural opportunities, is a tantalizing enigma. Perhaps they postpone everything, for five years later they brought a younger daughter, by then a high-school senior. who in vocabulary scored like the average fifth-grade pupil.

The Human Engineering Laboratory started in 1922 and has worked steadily to push its testing back to the younger ages; and yet, after more than twenty years of continuous effort, a few parents still wait until their extremely subjective son or daughter reaches junior or senior year of high school and confronts the discouraging impossibility of matriculating in some desired college. Extremely subjective children should be tested at age eight or nine, with additional tests every year from that time through college.

With a lengthy history of brain injury at birth, a sixteen-year-old tow-headed boy scored extremely subjective in personality, very low in accounting aptitude, and BRAIN equally low in English vocabulary. His anxious INJURY mother described the small, ungraded special room, in one of New York's huge coeducational public schools, to which her son had been assigned; but this is not equivalent to the small boys' school with a total enrollment of less than seventy pupils, indicated by low accounting aptitude. An unbroken series of medical reports agreed upon a PROBABLE injury; not one stated flatly its downright existence. The boy's educational misplacement alone explained his scholastic retardation, with no morbid complications.

Had this boy come without mention of physical defect, his scant English vocabulary would deny him annual promotion in any public school; and yet the boundary of his vocabulary showed every normal feature, lying merely among easy words instead of in the more advanced region. His first wrong answers, words barely eluding him, were opposites of the correct meaning, the final step in the learning process, just prior to full apprehension. His next errors were misleads used in the same circumstances as the test word but with different meanings; and so on through the normal learning process reversed. Incredible as it seems that a sixteen-year-old boy should be ignorant of such easy words as: APART, ASK, BUSHY, CONFERENCE, CUT, DAILY, SECRET, and UNTIDY, there is every scientific justification for believing that by starting where his present knowledge stops, he can build his vocabulary and with every additional word adjust more easily to life.

Science might passively diagnose his predicament as chronic brain injury; or facing the obstacles it might actively seek alleviation. The Laboratory elects this last point of view.

Tested at age nine, with a similar history of brain lesion, one boy lifted his English vocabulary in two and a quarter years from below the 5th percentile to the 36th, with the result that his parents concluded no defect existed and a bright-eyed youngster with no vestige of an earlier dullness continued to hold his normal place in school.

XVII

VOCABULARY VERSUS A TRADE

"But," asked the disquieted mother of a handicapped boy, "would it not be practical to learn a trade so that he can always support himself?" This pertinent question recurs at all stages of education. With the technical mutations of modern engineering, most trades disappear within a lifetime, or incredible changes render obsolete all previous specialized training; for skills are surprisingly narrowly limited to the minute task at which achieved. Despite the similarity of the finger-dexterity and the tweezer-dexterity boards, work-samples 16 and 18, which resemble one another more closely than two jobs, speed acquired in one is of no aid in performing the other. Granting the essential qualities of particularized knowledge, many boys score too low in their general English vocabulary to live normally in the civilized world of today; and the Laboratory believes additional words of more permanent value than a precarious trade which must ordinarily be abandoned and another learned by middle life, when its possessor lacks youthful enthusiasm and is perhaps supporting indigent parents instead of their helping him.

Age seventeen, with no confident grasp of his surroundings and with the concentration of a nine-year-old child, a tall, thin, red-polled youth resembled his mother in stature, in shape of head, and in general coloring; but he smiled vacuously as one desirous of perpetually pleasing. When the test administrator recommended that the boy concentrate on vocabulary building, this college-graduate mother replied that she and her husband must take a realistic viewpoint, explaining that her son scored low I.Q. and could not do school work, but must ultimately earn his own living. They felt in consequence that he should obtain immediate vocational training, and came to the Laboratory for aid in selecting the exact course.

Let us accept the mother's lead and seek a truly realistic program. She knows that her son scores low in a so-called general intelligence test, she does not know that he lacks intelligence; for one must face realistically two alternatives: the boy may lack general intelligence and in consequence score low, or he may possess intelligence and yet score low because of low accounting aptitude and low English vocabulary. The attempted acquisition of a trade to the exclusion of general background would lead this seventeen-year-old boy directly into a blind alley, for he scores below the 10th percentile in both finger dexterity, worksample 16, and tweezer dexterity, worksample 18, and equally low in structural visualization, giving little statistical chance in any manual or mechanical operation. In observation he scores above the median and so might seek employment as an inspector either in industry or with an insurance company; but routine inspection does not demand vocational training. What the mother terms a realistic view is in this instance tragically shortsighted.

Pursue for an equal distance the optimistic alternative, the possibility that the boy has intelligence but scores low for want of accounting aptitude and vocabulary. Many general intelligence tests contain a vocabulary section, with other parts dependent upon word meanings, so that a low-vocabulary boy is seriously handicapped. But an English vocabulary is always acquirable; and every word gained improves to that extent the score in the vocabulary sections of general intelligence tests; and without vocabulary men do not succeed later in life. Low accounting aptitude and low English vocabulary combined lead to the kind of school failure which the mother takes as further evidence of intellectual dullness. The boy looks blank, for he does not understand simple English remarks. His top measurable aptitude is analytical reasoning, a trait impossible to use without the knowledge background which the Laboratory calls vocabulary. The mother presupposes inability to acquire words; but her son already scores at the 14th percentile, and other boys below the 5th have improved.

To summarize: the assumption of low intelligence suggests vocational training, unsuitable for this boy; the alternative, inherent intelligence, conflicts with no known fact, requires additional general academic background with an ultimate chance of using analytical reasoning. Scholastic inability, an inevitable hurdle due to low accounting aptitude and low vocabulary, can be met, the first by a small school, the second by more words.

Aptitudes grow in the poorest soil, thrive without nourishment, need no cultivation. In a group of tragically underprivileged children the Laboratory found brilliant aptitude patterns, but no words; for knowledge needs environment. By definition, knowledge comes from daily companions, from teachers, from books. One might expect a slum environment, sickness, and lack of food, to stunt aptitude growth, and the Laboratory finds as yet no such evidence; but each unfavorable aspect retards knowledge. The boy who wants a fact to satisfy a moment's curiosity, to fill a gap in his own thought process, and has no book immediately at hand, loses a rare opportunity. One hears the so-called practical parent declare that if a boy is really interested he will go to the library and look it up. Examine this advice practically. A mediocre college graduate knows the meanings of perhaps one hundred thousand words; a brilliantly successful man, at the top of his profession, may know half again as many. But take the smaller figure. One hundred thousand trips to a public library, at the rate of one a day, require some three hundred years. Any boy forced to visit the town library for each new word learns slowly.

But the rationalizing parent again counters that he has a dictionary. The man at the top knows facts as well as words; it happens that word knowledge is easier to measure and a valuable facet of general background.

In the business world nearly half of the top executives, forty per cent in one study, are not college graduates but in rigid vocabulary tests show a mysterious breadth and exactness of word knowledge. Where this knowledge springs from or how it is nourished is as yet unknown; but no one worries about this irresistible group who rise uncared for. Another sixty per cent at the top of the business world, and probably a far greater per cent of the professions, work hard under formal tutelage for the knowledge they possess. Those who can afford the individual attention of a private school, followed by four years of college, can gain knowledge though it may come slowly and laboriously. But the boy who needs every bit of help he can be given, who is perpetually retarded by lack of books, may, even at the age of twelve or fifteen, be too old ever to gain the top of his profession.

For anyone limited seriously by space, reference books are probably the first to acquire. The out-of-print six or eight volumed CENTURY DICTIONARY is the backbone of every library. The Laboratory paid as little as sixteen dollars for its eight volumes. Odd editions of the ENCYCLOPEDIA BRITANNICA and of the child's BOOK OF KNOWLEDGE should be in every library. But these are not enough for any child who aspires to rise above the average of his profession; and the man's need is even greater for he has less time to squander. He must have a dozen books within easy reach on every subject he is likely to investigate. If he listens to radio music a dozen volumes on this subject alone are not enough. He should have books on operas, on symphonies, on program music and modern music, complete musical scores for Beethoven, Mozart, Tschaikowsky, and all standard compositions likely to be heard repeatedly, separate lives of all composers likely to be represented, three hundred volumes on music alone. Some may rest unopened for years, but should be there when wanted. One obstacle is of course the original cost; but used books are not expensive and the time which they take to find adds to the seeker's background. Space is another obstacle; and books are difficult to move for one who is not settled permanently. But lack of books, and the insistence that the last be read before another is bought, retards knowledge. The Laboratory recommends that books be read rapidly, rarely digested carefully, skimmed for the one or two ideas for which one happens to be prepared. Another book on the same subject by a different author adds a new idea, another scientific text adds a new technical term, another permanent part to one's working background. From every book each reader adds different words, different ideas, those next in order for which he is ready.

General reading adds to the richness of a word already known, shades its implications, but is time consuming in rapid vocabulary building, for no book appears in words of a single level only, and one reads many pages to stumble on the next word in order of difficulty.

XVIII

ENGLISH VOCABULARY LEVELS

English vocabulary grows exactly as a building rises, stone by stone, brick by brick, floor by floor, the foundation before the roof. To play an effective role in a readily workable language new words must be learned in their natural order, the easiest first. and then the more difficult, each resting on others beneath; for one of the Laboratory's startling discoveries is that words hold fixed places in a rigidly determinable sequence. Some, statistically discoverable through vocabulary tests, are known to virtually all adults, and to conserve learning time should be known to the individual student prior to others less familiar to the general public. One who laboriously commits to memory some hard word before the easy ones, remembers it only momentarily and largely squanders his labor. The boy who memorizes some unusual word must carry it consciously in mind, with little or no chance to use it naturally, until the rest of his vocabulary catches up, like a brick layer who holds a selected brick high in the air until the wall rises to its height.

Short words are in general slightly easier than long ones and should ordinarily be learned first. Anglo-Saxon words are as a whole easier than those of Latin origin, and these in turn easier than others from Greek. Old words, those dating from early in the history of the language, are generally easier than words of more recent origin. But none of these rules is accurate enough to be a practical guide to effective, rapid learning. The only certain figure is the percentage of examinees who miss the word in a controlled test. In the JOHNSON O'CONNOR ENGLISH VOCABULARY BUILDER, eleven hundred carefully studied words appear in the order of their statistical difficulty, in the order in which they should be learned. While few in number compared with the many thousand of a small dictionary, these eleven hundred form a solid trunk from which grow interlacing branches as the learner hears other words, adding each where it belongs.

The introduction to the VOCABULARY BUILDER advises turning to that section of the book in which the words seem doubtful. Experience proves that this procedure too often leaves an unfilled gap. Though it wastes some time, a sounder practice is for each student to begin at the first word, HORSESHOER, and to read two a day in order from that point on. With children who show any tendency to reading troubles, parents should read the two words aloud.

To measure improvement from year to year, vocabulary-test forms with different first letters must always be used, as forms AD, BC, CC, DB, and EB. In the Laboratory's nomenclature, the second letter designates the revision. Thus form BA was made by replacing, in each item of form B, the mislead, or incorrect choice, marked least frequently by the population as a whole. A statistical analysis based on the administration of the new form BA, and again replacing the unattractive, or least-frequently-marked misleads, resulted in form BB, and this in turn led to form BC, a third revision of the original.

The original plan to build strictly comparable forms has proved impossible, for with each revision the difficulty of a form changes slightly, and separate items move in comparison with other forms, so that the first items of one form may be easier than another, and the subsequent items harder. Instead of parallel forms, the Laboratory now converts each score on each separate form to a common general vocabulary scale. This allows a student to take worksample 95, form BC, at the beginning of the school year, and form CC, or any other, at the close, and by converting each to the same scoring scale evaluate improvement.

The detailed accomplishments of a vocabulary-building, college freshman class of twenty-five, which did not use the VOCABULARY BUILDER, show what can be done by intensive educational techniques. At the beginning of the school year the lowest student scored 57 correct words on worksample

95, form BA, now revised to form BC. Reference to page 120, table XXII, of Unsolved Business Problems, shows that a so-called raw score of 57 correct answers on form B, or on any of its revisions such as form BA, equals a general scale score of 84. Turning next to page 58 of Aptitudes and the Languages, figure 8 gives 89 on the general scale as the median score for seventh-grade pupils. Thus the lowest student in this vocabulary-building college freshman class started the year five points below the normal seventh-grade pupil. In the same class, the top raw score was 128 correct words on form BA, equivalent to 172 on the general scale, according to table XXII of Unsolved Business Problems, six points higher than 166, the median college senior, figure 8 of Aptitudes and the Languages. To the experienced college professor who gave this course, a warm personal friend of the author, it seemed incredible that one of his students showed less exact knowledge of English words than the average seventh-grade pupil, another, also classed as a college freshman, more word knowledge than the typical college senior. Such students, working together in the same room, with the same text, hearing the same lectures, do not learn at maximum speed.

At the opening of college this freshman class, which scattered from 84 to 172 on the general scale, averaged 129, two points below the high-school junior level. In May, at the end of the college year, the same group averaged 143, between the 138 average for high-school seniors, and 147 for college freshmen. In one college year the group improved from just below high-school juniors to well above high-school seniors. The normal gain from junior to senior year of high school is 7 points on the general scale, from senior year of high school to freshman year of college, 9 points. This vocabulary-building group improved 14 points.

In studying such improvement, the scores of all students who fail to complete must be omitted from the study both at the beginning and at the end of the year, for low-vocabulary students frequently leave during the term. Inclusion of their low scores at the beginning of the course but not at the end, when they have dropped, lowers the original average and so makes the improvement appear greater than it actually is.

For vividness vocabulary scores may be expressed in terms of vocational levels, as shown in table xxx, page 134, of the Too-Many-Aptitude Woman, based on mature men and women, approximately forty years of age. To make the comparison fair, scores of younger people must be increased to the scores they will probably attain at age forty, assuming normal improvement in the interim. The bottom girl in the college freshman class, with a general scale score of 84 at age 20, should score about 100 at age 40. This is below the average of any occupational group the Laboratory has studied. Individuals of course score as low as this college freshman; but as a group grocery clerks score above her, averaging 135, shipping clerks average 138.

The top boy in the class, with a general scale score of 172, should at age 40 score about 206, figure 6, page 52, Aptitudes and the Languages. Lawyers average 209. Individuals in this college freshman class scattered from the seventh-grade level to college senior, from the grocery-clerk level to the lawyer.

The class average (medium) of 129 on the general scale at age 20 is equivalent to 155 at age 40. as shown by figure 6, pages 52 and 53, of Aptitudes and the Languages, a score between that of department-store sales clerks and insurance salesmen, table xxx, page 134, of the Too-Many-Aptitude Woman. The higher score of 143, made by this group at the end of the school year, is equivalent to about 173 at age 40. This group should climb 7 to 9 points per year and actually climbed 14, a gain of 5 to 7 points, equivalent to about half the vocabulary rise from a mechanic to a machinist, or from a department-store sales clerk to a stenographer.

The bottom girl, with a vocabulary equivalent to the average seventh-grade level, failed other courses and left the university by request at the end of freshman year. The top student improved a normal 9 points but not the 14 of the class. In every such group the level of instruction caters to the average; so that those above and below this point gain less than those between, and to progress rapidly must educate themselves rather than depend on classroom instruction. The Vocabulary Builder is designed to overcome this situation by allowing each pupil to work independently at his own level.

This metropolitan university does not countenance segregating students by vocabulary or academic level, because of the stigma attached to the low group. But if the extremes are ever to make maximum progress. education must attack this problem intellectually and find some way of teaching the high and low separately without making the latter feel inferior.

Many low-vocabulary students score high in isolated aptitudes, such as structural visualization, and with a high structural professor could do brilliant geometry, physics, and geology. Could each low-vocabulary pupil. high in structural visualization, be assigned simultaneously to the top physics section and the bottom vocabulary section much of the low-vocabulary taint would go. One inevitable danger must be avoided; because high-vocabulary pupils do well in a majority of academic subjects as English, history, Latin, and the languages, school executives assume they should do equally well in structural subjects and criticize structurally gifted faculty members for deviating in their evaluation. To gain the desirable end a course must be so constructed that only high structural students keep the pace and high vocabulary alone fails. Then only does ability to hold a place in an exact science compensate for membership in the low-vocabulary section.

Another boy or girl, low in structural visualization but high in tonal memory, can gain similar satisfaction by excelling in professional music; and still a third, high in memory for design, can excel in art. These inherent aptitudes, structural visualization, tonal memory, and memory for design, are unaffected by education. They are strengthening nuclei around which education can build; but they are not its goal, for vocabulary alone is acquirable.

A possibility which might be tried is that of labeling each vocabulary section by a different subject matter. A group assigned to a section called: Vocabularies of Science might be lifted rapidly far above the school level in exact knowledge of technical terms, and simultaneously be taught general English vocabulary at a low level, without feeling in any way inferior, for boys high in structural visualization, who often score appallingly low in their grasp of ordinary English words, may enjoy science enough to acquire the lingo of physics, astronomy, geology, or meteorology. Other sections labeled: Vocabulary of Art, Vocabulary of Music, Vocabulary of Literature, might start at different general levels. Whatever the emotional disturbances involved, some solution must be found; for maximum progress comes only in teaching each boy at his own vocabulary level.

The extremely subjective person often rebels at raising the general level of his background, but builds with pleasure some specialized knowledge. An extremely subjective, mild spoken, naval lieutenant, planning his return to civilian life, scored at the 17th percentile in English vocabulary, above sixteen per cent of men his age. When urged to improve, he said he had always been too much the perfectionist to try new words and perhaps use them incorrectly, a normal subjective reaction. He was happier keeping to the few he knew well, where he was confident of the pronunciation. He could not quite bring himself to try the unknown, though he realized it might mean progress. Yet against this generally low background, he scored surprisingly high in two special fields, navigation and the fine arts. He had been in the navy some three and a half years, but in the technical terms of navigation, about which he had known nothing a few years earlier, he scored at the 90th percentile. When questioned he said that his assignment was to master navigation. The field was small enough so that there seemed some hope of perfection. He could be reasonably certain of each word before trying it. His instructor in navigation knew enough to explain his errors, to appreciate his slips, and never laugh at his mistakes.

Before enlisting he had been casually interested in art, in an amateurish way, read something in the field, owned art books, and to his amazement he scored equally high, at the 90th percentile in the Laboratory's technical vocabulary of art terms, worksample 275, with no idea that he had acquired more knowledge than the average general reader. How wide are those two acquired towers? The Laboratory should have continued with other adjacent knowledge tests. Does his grasp of aesthetic terms include a knowledge of paintings as measured by worksample 183? Is this aesthetic knowledge wide enough to include music, together with its history, versification, and literature, as measured by worksamples 286, 295, 405, 288, and 293? Does his knowledge of navigation embrace a vocabulary of mathematics, or of physics, as measured by worksamples 280 and 181? To enable it to plot a clear profile of knowledge, and so plan further reading, to strengthen and broaden such strong spots, the Laboratory believes in additional periodic appointments.

A so-called first appointment, whether a single lasting three hours, or a double composed of two sessions on different days, sets the vocational direction by an inventory of inherent aptitudes. Subsequent appointments, which the Laboratory believes should follow one each year, measure primarily knowledge, which, more than aptitudes, determines how far one goes.

In choosing between a shallow breadth and deep specialization, the extremely subjective perfectionist should establish himself as an instituted authority, mastering his subject by a combination of hard work and the exclusion of ramifications, for no one excels in all knowledge. In his general English vocabulary, a delightful conversationalist scored at the 85th percentile, among the top fifteen persons in every hundred, a score which the Laboratory grades A and calls high. But the man disparaged his own progress, for extreme subjectivity aspires to that level of accomplishment set by Francis Galton in his study of eminence, the topmost man in four thousand, in the top fortieth of the top percentile.

In subversion of this occupational pinnacle, the materialist advances the mathematical impossibility of every boy's climbing, for percentiles are relative ranks. Undeniably not all boys can ascend all peaks; but in four thousand specialities four thousand different boys can each gain the top of one, and this must be the goal of every extremely subjective person.

The extremely subjective person gains one by one a number of specialized technical vocabularies more felicitously than a broad smattering background. With a given amount of work narrowly focused he mounts more quickly above the general level, to a point where he is no longer open to public ridicule for mistakes. By building one restricted subject beside another the extremely subjective man gains breadth gradually and ultimately the high general knowledge essential to success.

On the other hand, opposed to the practice of building one tower, bits of evidence indicate that a general groundwork of knowledge is laid more economically than too tall a tower, which like upended bricks piled on top of one another needs finally a broader base to prevent toppling. Whenever the Laboratory feels that such advice will not be too disheartening, it recommends fundamental courses in English composition, English literature, mathematics, and especially Latin, as a solid foundation for extensive English vocabulary building, rather than specialized vocational courses which too frequently draw the adult because they seem immediately applicable. With no more than eighth-grade education, the financial secretary to a wealthy man, who as she expressed it did not want to be bothered with details, scored spectacularly high in number memory which she was probably not using. Had the Laboratory recommended a fresh start in a new direction, the average examinee would have left delighted, having come with the prevision of just such a discovery. But her complete results included:

very high (95th percentile)	number memory,
average to high	creative imagination,
average (52nd percentile)	accounting aptitude,
extremely subjective	personality,
low (28th percentile)	English vocabulary.

One so low in this last cannot sense the full horizon of any job and after a few years in a new place reaches another dead end. With accounting aptitude at the 52nd percentile, this understanding woman made an assured position for herself; but with vocabulary at the 28th percentile could not recognize the unbounded opportunities within sight. With considerable trepidation the test administrator advised her to continue where she was and, because she gave undoubted satisfaction, to ask for the special privilege of studying specified hours each week. She approached the near-by university, discovered that courses could be taken by one at the age of thirty-four with no high-school diploma, learned what hours they were held, and presented her employer with a tentative program.

To her amazement she found outlet for her high number memory, a characteristic of stockmarket traders, in scheduling her employer's investments, which she had never before realized might fall under her keen supervision.

XIX

OVER–VERBALIZATION

To this pertinacious stress on English vocabulary, a trite reaction expresses the conviction that the vulgar populace is already over-educated, that verbalization is not education, an attitude substantiated by sporadic case histories. For sheer adventure a high-school boy went to sea at mid-term of junior year, taking all the books he could tote. With the outbreak of the world war and the requisition of experienced seamen, he remained aship long after the novelty wore threadbare; but with every home-port call he restocked his cramped cabin with fresh literature. At the age of twenty-six, after ten sea years, he scored above ninety per cent of college graduates in word knowledge; but he displayed an astounding ignorance of urban life. With him, bookishness unquestionably outstripped social adjustment.

Teachers cry over-verbalization because they see foreign words memorized as dissociated lists; but with an overwhelming preponderance of the metropolitan population variegated experiences pile up more rapidly than words to name them; for modern civilization rains impressions, while the naming process lags behind. The automobile penetrates inaccessible parts known once only to the native. The airplane, the movies, and the radio, carry the child further afield; and these passing appearances must be labeled to be savored.

The popular epithet OVER-EDUCATED applies to men with more academic knowledge than is needed in their daily jobs, but who at the same time possess too little to reach the next rung of their own vocational ladder.

A truer term is UNDER-EDUCATED. A thirty-year-old plasterer's assistant graded in the top quarter in three aptitudes, above the 90th percentile in structural visualization, high in both ideaphoria and accounting aptitude, and objective in personality, an architectural combination of inherent traits. In exact word knowledge, he outstrips a third of college graduates, far above the level of his plaster carrying, but not enough for architectural design where he belongs. Worldly advice suggests his rising to master plasterer before troubling himself about the next step; but the Laboratory believes that one should not lightly expend time and energy for a distant goal without prospect of permanent satisfaction. Skilled plastering is no easily acquired trade and offers insufficient outlet for either ideaphoria or high vocabulary. Also it is no nearer true architecture, where he belongs. The man might of course start at the bottom in an architect's office; but the profession employs the compound structural visualization plus ideaphoria only of men with freedom of expression at the top. An English vocabulary little higher than the lowest third of college men is not enough to assure him greater challenge in architecture than his present job, where he earns substantially more than an architect's apprentice. Visionary or far-sighted counsel, according to its wisdom, says continue as plasterer's helper at an adequate wage, studying architecture intensively, reading discriminatively, bothering with drafting only as a desirable tool, for the drawing board seldom compensates for ideaphoria or objectivity, and awaiting one of those rare opportunities, which do occur, some sort of association with an architect who glimpses hidden capabilities.

Granted the requisite aptitudes, no man has too much knowledge; for vocabulary determines the distance traveled, after aptitudes point the way. The high-vocabulary man who goes a wrong direction succeeds beyond himself, goes further than one would expect from a knowledge of his born capacity, a fact misinterpreted as demonstrating that knowledge shows lack of suitable ability, inappropriate aptitudes giving the impression of excessive education. The difficulty is a wrong first direction, not undue vocabulary.

Like any priceless asset a large and exact English vocabulary colors calculations. To a nursery governess, impatient with her menial station, tired of endless hours, limited freedom, and the fretful impact of noisy children, the test administrator offered factory inspection of delicate instruments as using observation and to a limited extent tweezer dexterity; for the woman scored:

high	in observation,
high	in tweezer dexterity,
extremely subjective	in personality,
and above the median, grade B,	in vocabulary.

Regular factory routine, practical advice which the woman sought, gives liberty for subjectivity to seek its shell when human pressure becomes unbearable.

But to three staff members, who subsequently reviewed the case, the expedient change held scant hope of permanent happiness. Already too high in vocabulary to rest for long at instrument inspection, industrial promotion would soon carry her to supervision where her extremely subjective personality would lead to more friction than in the nursery. If she refused the executive branch, she would move to more highly skilled mechanical work and, with a vocabulary already equivalent to that of the average man in engineering, she would be dissatisfied with anything of less consequence; but here low structural visualization would make ultimate success unlikely. Factory inspection offers momentary relief but less future than her present position as nurserymaid.

High observation, high tweezer dexterity, and extreme subjectivity, suggest microscopy in some non-structural field, as perhaps bacteriology. While most laboratory technicians are college trained, and this woman held no diploma, she scored as high in vocabulary as the average college graduate. The reconsidered advice was:

1. That she keep her present position despite momentary restlessness.

2. That she buy inexpensive, used books on the microscope and its handling.

3. That she rent or buy a good scientific microscope.

4. That she interest her charges in the multitude of minute life which one can study under the microscope, although her own low ideaphoria made this prospect difficult to sense.

5. That both for their further education and her own she take her charges to museums where microscopic life can be seen, for her present work gave an ideal opportunity to interest them in the microscope and simultaneously to learn herself.

6. That she buy, perhaps from the General Biological Supply House in Chicago, a colony of living ants and set it up either in her own room or in the nursery.

7. That she obtain a balanced aquarium.

8. That she study her own duties carefully to see just how much actual freedom she could obtain and then start a college course in a nearby university.

To her amazement she found the austere parents of her obstreperous charges sympathetic and constructively helpful.

XX

CONCLUSION

In marking synonyms in an English vocabulary test an erudite college president, who read omnivorously, balked mulishly at guessing GLABROUS. He had never seen that combination of letters and averred that the inclusion of remote knowledge vitiated an otherwise inspiring testing program. A month later he addressed an apologetic open letter to the entire staff. Since his test appointment, he had met GLABROUS on three occasions, first in a newspaper editorial, then in a magazine article, and again in its strictly botanical sense, evidence, he declared unabashed, that he had passed the word repeatedly but, as he phrased it, been too ignorant to pause. Like this college president, many persons leave the Laboratory dissatisfied both with the actual results and with the manner of their presentation. Harried examinees come for help and feel cheated on leaving with a list of plain scores, percentiles, and letter grades, plotted like hieroglyphics on a mysterious bargraph, meaningless without the accompanying printed book of some hundred pages which must next be read.

The bargraph, built line by line in the course of the testing session, represents as many of the eighteen aspects, table LXII, of the individual as can be measured in the restricted time. In a single appointment this ordinarily amounts to four or five separate aptitudes; in a double appointment to ten or twelve. The remaining aptitudes the Laboratory measures in a series of recurrent appointments, one each year after the first, at the same time remeasuring English vocabulary and so plotting annual knowledge gained; for one not previously tested must re-

TABLE LXII

EIGHTEEN APTITUDES WHICH THE LABORATORY REGARDS AS SUFFICIENTLY INDEPENDENT OF ONE ANOTHER TO HAVE SOME CHANCE OF SURVIVING AS UNITARY TRAITS

1. PERSONALITY — Word Association: The distinction between the objective born group-mixer and the extremely subjective individualist; in the vocational world the distinction between the typical sales or business executive type, and the unique artist, musician, scientist, or writer.
2. ACCOUNTING APTITUDE — Number Checking: Instinctive clerical, paper-and-pencil, speed and accuracy.
3. STRUCTURAL VISUALIZATION — Wiggly Block, Formboard, Black Cube, and Pyramid: A mental imaging of solid forms, seeing in three dimensions, as opposed to ABSTRACT VISUALIZATION, dealing with intangible ideas.
4. FINGER DEXTERITY — Pin Board: A self-defining trait.
5. TWEEZER DEXTERITY — Pin Board with Tweezers: Facility in handling small, delicate instruments, in the use of tools.
6. GRIP — Dynamometer: A rough indication of physical strength, stamina.
7. MUSCULAR SPEED — Tapping: A measurable and independent characteristic the significance of which is not yet understood.
8. INDUCTIVE REASONING — Three Pictures of One Type: Ability to sense a common element in some heterogeneous assortment, a gift for discovering a fundamental law.
9. ANALYTICAL REASONING — Boards for Word Arrangement: A gift for organizing material, for logical arrangement.
10. OBSERVATION — A Dozen Photographs of Numerous Common Objects: The trait measured is self-defining.

11. NUMBER MEMORY — Numbers on Motion-Picture Screen: A kind of visual memory independent of memory for design and also of tonal memory.

12. TONAL MEMORY — Dr. Carl E. Seashore's Phonograph Record: A gift approximating that which is ordinarily regarded as musical ability.

13. PITCH DISCRIMINATION — Dr. Carl E. Seashore's Phonograph Record: More than the ability to hear correctly a difference in pitch between two close notes, a niceness of sense perception.

14. PROPORTION APPRAISAL — Plates of Four Line Drawings: A worksample in which those who handle things score high, and those who handle abstract concepts score low.

15. MEMORY FOR DESIGN — Plates of Designs for Drawing from Memory: A characteristic of cartoonists and others who must draw from memory.

16. VISION — Formerly called VISUAL IMAGINATION — Simple Drawings which Suggest Ideas: An ability to see a distant goal with sufficient clarity to spend unproductive years in preparation.

17. IDEAPHORIA — Formerly called CREATIVE IMAGINATION — Writing for Ten Minutes on an Imaginative Theme: A trait used in advertising, selling, and teaching.

18. EYEDNESS — Card with a Hole: An indication of handedness or sidedness.

gard a first appointment as the initial step in a long series leading toward a fuller, richer, more unified existence.

The choice of a life's work, either in business or in the hazardous arts, should result from tranquil thought, not from a few minutes' hasty consideration. Compared with the former absurdly inadequate page and a half typed report, which often for brevity mentioned a single occupation or profession and in consequence led to numerous misinterpretations and wrong applications, the present interpretive reference book may list under a single aptitude a hundred or more alternatives. For persons who feel that a book of this size is cumbrous, laborious to peruse, that the Laboratory gives too much material to digest, there is no simple answer to life's problems. A single pre-

cept may suffice the child age nine, who can return a year
later for more. But with the older person, the Laboratory presents the facts at its disposal in this brochure, and in others of
the series, and burdens the examinee with the final determination, knowing that one who reaches his own decision cleaves
to it and rises more certainly than one who accepts a proffered
opinion until he trips on another equally plausible.

The Laboratory could undoubtedly give greater immediate
satisfaction by making its suggestions more specific and by
demanding less study of the examinee. But no amount of latent
ability succeeds without lavish effort. A vocational decision
which is too concrete is often superficial, leaving the deceptive
impression of an assured future which one need but sit passively
and await patiently.

This booklet which interprets the bargraph also warns of
exceptions which disturb not only the general public, un-
familiar with technical details, but to an equal extent the
research department. Among one hundred bank employees,
eighty per cent graded *A* in accounting aptitude, but the vice-
president who arranged the appointments graded *D*. Instead
of losing interest, the awkward finding, which worried the
Laboratory, gave him added confidence in test results; he
still wanted a majority of his employees to grade *A*, but he
felt that while clerical speed and accuracy are of vital importance throughout an organization, too strict adherence to
detail may handicap the man at the top; and moreover he
asserted that the guiding head of any large organization should
have qualities which the Laboratory cannot yet measure.
Aptitude testing is still in the research stage, where one must
gage what it has to give and accept the anomaly as a challenge
toward further understanding.

In another instance an executive engineer, graduate of a
celebrated technological institution, scheduled test appointments for fifty engineers, anticipating the results would aid
in guiding their futures to greater fruition. As a first natural
step he himself took the tests. He scored low in structural
visualization, where designing engineers score high, and extremely subjective in personality, where executives score
objective. Had this man come as a schoolboy, the Laboratory

would undoubtedly have advised against engineering, where he had unquestionably succeeded, and against executive work, where he held an enviable position.

Judging by his own results he impulsively canceled the fifty appointments, an attitude occasionally taken, certainly justifiable, but not the complete answer. Only two men in a hundred who grade D in structural visualization earn a steady living in engineering, but these two are exactly as successful as those who grade A. If the exception happens to be an underling the outcome is accepted and test results continue to be used constructively, but if the exception is a top man a testing program often stops abruptly, for he reasons that he at least ought to fit, even if others do not. Exceptions are rare but when they occur may be strikingly successful because they follow no rule, or sometimes because their very ineptness imposes hard work, which after all is the major part of success.

Nine men in every ten who go in a wrong direction fail to meet the challenge and drop by the way. Why the rare exception mounts the hurdle and rises to greater success because of obstacles overcome is as yet an unknown factor. The Laboratory believes the risk too great for the ordinary mortal; also that even the exception might have gone in the right direction and erected equal obstacles to challenge his strength by setting his goal sufficiently high, for no one yet has ever attained the ultimate apex of human capabilities.

Occasionally an occupied father writes that he has no time to read an elaborate report and demands a one or two page digest. When so busy, he should allow his son to plan his own life, for a boy's future calls for hours of consideration. Parents who expect a single magic word are inevitably disappointed, for life is by definition alive.

An intellectual man of twenty-eight, with an assured social and family background, graduated from medical school successfully, obtained his M.D., but after two and a half years of private practice found medicine so distasteful that he considered leaving the field. He scored:

high (93d percentile)   English vocabulary, and
low (30th percentile)   structural visualization.

Statistically the Laboratory advises those who score low in structural visualization against structural fields such as medicine, for difficulty with anatomy eliminates during freshman year of medical school most of those who score in this section. But the 30th percentile, while ranked low, is near enough the critical point between the 50th and 51st percentiles so that one person in twenty, or thereabouts, who scores here actually possesses this engineer's trait. Also an English vocabulary at the 93d percentile correlates with success in every direction and carries one over otherwise insurmountable obstacles; but does not make structural work agreeable when faced many hours a day. Yet had the Laboratory tested this quiet man earlier it would hesitate to decry medicine too vehemently. Only the individual, and not the Laboratory, knows how much a structural field means emotionally and whether or not the chance of one in twenty is worth taking.

His dissatisfaction with medicine may be low structural visualization, may be low inductive reasoning which he found essential in actual practice, but is more probably idle musical traits, tonal memory and pitch discrimination, for he loved music, played the violin for his own tranquil enjoyment, sang in his school and college glee clubs, and expected to continue through life; but he started medical practice during the world war, when from the outset he worked long, hectic hours, with no leisure, and though he had never thought of music as essential, an unused 100th-percentile tonal memory leads more often to failure than the lack of structural visualization and inductive reasoning.

Unsuitable knowledge and training combined with an internally conflicting aptitude pattern is likely to be a second-rate compromise. For this man the solution involves turning away from structural medicine, away from surgery and fractures, perhaps toward psychiatry, using the complementary trait, abstract visualization. An objection is the lack of inductive reasoning, essential also in non-structural diagnostic medicine. An investigation into the therapeutic effects of music might combine medical knowledge, worksample 323, in which this man made a nearly perfect score, with tonal memory and pitch discrimination. Or since these last two traits characterize

photographers, medical photography of some sort, possibly
X-ray work, might be a solution, although the actual making
of X-rays requires little medical knowledge and their interpretation takes structural visualization.

Those who expect the Laboratory to give some pat decision
and who criticize the present policy, a bare tabulation of
scores together with an explanatory book of this size, forcing
either the examinee or parents to spend several hours studying
the findings, should recall this man who spent hard years in
medical school and hospital work to reach a profession he
came to abhor. An earlier test, and a comparatively few hours
devoted to interpreting the results, might have saved wasted
years, the cost of a medical school education, and possible un-
happiness later. A majority of persons come for aptitude and
knowledge measurements; and, though the Laboratory realizes
that the tabulated results are often but a fragment of the total
situation, the appointment time is so short compared with the
problems of life that to do its own job at all adequately, it
must limit itself to measurements and their interpretation, and
sedulously avoid any temptation to go outside its own field.

Eighteen separate mental elements combine in two hundred
and sixty thousand different ways, over which the Human
Engineering Laboratory has no control. Each of these, ideally,
calls for a different type of work. Less probably than one per
cent, not more than a few hundred combinations, point clearly
in known directions which can be named by single words: law,
medicine, engineering, writing. For the others no test administrator, regardless of skill, can glance at a bargraph and describe
exactly the work it indicates. For real happiness one should
integrate all of one's aptitudes toward a common goal. But for
the moment consider only two of the total eighteen, and neglect
the other accompanying ones. The combination high structural
visualization with extreme subjectivity, shown by one-eighth
of examinees, means technical engineering; the reverse, low
structural visualization and objectivity, another three-eighths
of examinees, means with equal clarity executive work, management, supervision. High structural visualization coupled with
objectivity, still another three-eighths of examinees, appears
in architecture and in work called with not much exactness

DEVELOPMENT ENGINEERING. For approximately seven-eighths of tested examinees, the Laboratory has some sort of concrete, corroborated suggestion facilitating the interpretation.

The remaining combination of these two elements behooves with less decisiveness; and the test administrator turns elsewhere for guidance. High accounting aptitude, in this final eighth of low structural visualization and extreme subjectivity, calls for certified public accounting; high ideaphoria and high inductive reasoning for writing. But there remains a slim section of the population for whom the Laboratory has as yet no set specific.

The history of many persons with an unorthodox pattern is repeated failure at successive conventional tasks. Among the letters from this small group, which express no more disappointment than the test administrator feels in the result, a father writes that, after trying numerous jobs himself without finding what he regards as his rightful place in the modern world, he is determined that his daughter shall not go through life with similar unrequited groping. She scores extremely subjective in personality, low in structural visualization, low in ideaphoria, but at the 100th percentile in analytical reasoning, a pattern which does not fit perfectly into teaching, medicine, law, or any hackneyed type of graduate training. Yet the father demands the name of some trite field in order that the girl may avoid his own restlessness, and in so doing unwittingly drives her toward a facsimile of his own past. She lacks the ideaphoria of the teacher and is unlikely to be happy in formal education; and yet shows perfect analytical reasoning, the teacher's gift for organizing material. She lacks the clerical speed of the accountant but shows his feeling for arranging an audit. She should collect an extensive library on editorial techniques and educational methods, seeking a problem which calls for more than normal analytical reasoning, without taxing too heavily either ideaphoria or inductive reasoning. The examinee whose aptitude pattern fails to coincide with any standard undertaking finds it economical of time to give up the notion of fitting neatly some designated niche, and face this nonconformity rather than await its ubiquity through wasted years of tossing about.

A tall, quiet, assembly-department foreman does not belong where he is in a war plant, for he scores extremely subjective in personality and low in structural visualization; but no recognized field uses his combination:

average to high (65th percentile)	proportion appraisal,
average to high (60th percentile)	accounting aptitude,
average to high (60th percentile)	number memory,
extremely subjective	personality, and
high (80th percentile)	English vocabulary.

The proportion-appraisal test is not yet well enough authenticated to warrant his turning suddenly to art even were he well informed. Certified public accounting, suggested by his accounting aptitude and extreme subjectivity, would not use his proportion appraisal or number memory; and the higher aspects of accounting, to which he should rise because of his high vocabulary, use analytical reasoning which he lacks; and still further his 60th-percentile accounting aptitude is hardly high enough to justify gambling years of accounting training. Number memory suggests production planning, expediting, chasing; but here advancement comes to objectivity. Pressed for a direct, immediate answer the Laboratory can only state that any sudden shift seems a mistake and advise that he remain exactly where he is.

But this is not the whole answer. One who expects the full benefit of aptitude tests must absorb all the Laboratory knows about aptitudes and then work his own calm way toward their integration. In this case the man should build around his proportion appraisal a library of art, where he can pick up innumerable books from the second-hand shops, and where there is every chance of his gaining restful enjoyment though he never gains enough knowledge to enter art, for one who scores high in vocabulary enjoys reaching into a subject of which he knows little, entering a new country. This factory foreman should build an equally extensive library around his accounting aptitude, purchasing used books on accounting, on the theory of banking, on statistics and actuarial studies; and still a third library around number memory with books on production control, production planning and scheduling. As these three collections expand, like widening circles from three stones dropped in still water, they must ultimately touch and finally overlap. In the tiny region common to all three lies the future of this man; and until he finds it he can live a more comfortable and secure life, with greater financial freedom, exactly where he is. He tranquilly assumed the responsibility of cultivating three new subjects, two of which, accounting and production control, he ought to know for his present work.

From a first appointment comes any one of a dozen indications, each the start of a year's work; the need of a strengthened English vocabulary, further training of the left hand, exercise of a hitherto neglected aptitude, experience in writing, transfer to a small school, the study of Latin. Members of the staff strive persistently to bridge the gap between aptitude scores and practical decisions; but even could the Laboratory place each examinee in precisely the right job its real task would be no more than started, for a test appointment is only a beginning, an inventory of such aptitudes and types of knowledge as the Laboratory can now measure, on which a plan for the future can be built.

As the frank college president blindly overlooked GLABROUS, so countless others leave priceless opportunities unheeded. The distressed mortal who feels that life glides past while he stands still is almost always unequipped to recognize the precious minor options which would have carried him far had he chosen correctly at each intersection. For this reason the Human Engineering Laboratory does not regard a test appointment as settling an imminent decision no matter how vital; its ambition is not the temporary solution of a momentary problem, but rather furnishing factual data on which to build a program toward self-expression and a richer life, an effort to give every examinee a lasting understanding of himself so that he will recognize opportunities much as the college president became aware of a new word which he had no doubt seen but disregarded, for the achievement of happiness is rarely spectacular, but rather the result of a perpetual series of minor correct decisions, over a period of years, each swinging life's course another quarter point toward the ideal.

SELECTION OF COLLEGE

With eminent men and women sponsoring with equal insistence two diametrically opposed theories of education, neither side can legitimately be declared either entirely right or wholly wrong. The Human Engineering Laboratory believes in the further education of every human being, not in the selective education of a few. With negligible exceptions, it believes that every one of the hundred and forty million citizens of the United States would be individually more richly successful, and of greater world value, if possessed of broader and more exact knowledge.

An eclectic group, chosen for further education perhaps because easy to teach, does not lift the masses with it, but rises above, leaving a gap between itself and the populace. When this separation becomes apparent, the world sloughs off the select, leaving the whole where it was before. To educate the entire population economically and effectively, each person must start at his own level and progress from that point on. This belief rests on the Laboratory's work with English vocabulary.

English words form a natural order of difficulty, from easy words to more difficult ones. In the Laboratory's various vocabulary tests, a large percentage of persons mark easy words correctly, while but few know the difficult words. The same order of difficulty reappears in the testing of various populations ranging from four hundred persons to a thousand.

This finding depends upon the percentage of persons who know, or fail to know, each word; only by measuring a number of people can the Laboratory thus arrange words.

The second finding relates to the individual. With words in order as just described, each person knows most of the meanings to a point where his or her vocabulary becomes doubtful and knows few beyond this point.

This suggests that all persons learn new words in the same order. Some know easy words only, and none beyond. Others know easy and average words, but not the difficult ones. With a few exceptions, no one tested knows hard words without knowing also the preliminary easy ones. The exceptions are foreign students, familiar with Latin, French, or Italian, but ignorant of Anglo-Saxon, who in consequence interpret correctly difficult English words of Latin origin, without knowing English words familiar to every native child. In planning American education, such exceptions should be ignored or regarded as separate issues. For the average American, whether boy or girl or adult, it is ordinarily a waste of time to teach laboriously a difficult word before the easier ones are known. Words should be taught in their order of difficulty. This means that students at different vocabulary levels cannot be taught effectively and economically together.

Under present conditions, widely divergent vocabulary levels meet together in the same class, hear the same lectures, read the same texts, try to do the same assignments. In nearly every college freshman class an occasional student scores as low as the average seventh grade pupil in the Laboratory's English vocabulary tests; while other students, of approximately the same age, score not only above the average college graduate, but measurably above the average faculty member. This represents a spread of two grammar-school years, four high-school years, and four college years, between the lowest vocabulary and the highest. A majority of low-vocabulary freshmen fail, while many of the very high ones leave college without graduating. Students who score at different points in the vocabulary scale should not be taught together in the same class, or even in the same school. In line with this belief, the Laboratory recommends different colleges to different vocabulary levels.

The immediate problem is one which the Laboratory evaded for years, the practical selection of specific colleges at each vocabulary level. Naturally the Laboratory thought first of averaging the freshman vocabularies in each school where it has an indicative number; but found less difference between one college and another than it needs to start each student at his own level. At time of entrance the freshmen in one college averaged, in the Laboratory's English vocabulary tests, 129 on the general scale, just below the average high-school junior. In another college the freshmen averaged 170 on the same general scale, just above 166, the average for college seniors. These are averages, for in both colleges individual students ranged from the seventh-grade level to above the average faculty member. This gave a six-year educational spread between colleges at present, and well over a ten-year spread is needed to start each high-school graduate at his own level.

Next the Laboratory sought a present tendency which might be exaggerated; in general old colleges average slightly higher in vocabulary than more recently founded ones. This might perhaps be anticipated. Most old schools are better known than newer ones. Their names are more familiar, and they attract, for this reason, more applicants, and so have greater choice. Such scholastic selection correlates with English vocabulary; and in consequence the greater the selection the higher in general the vocabulary level. To extend this apparent tendency the Laboratory decided to recommend the oldest colleges of the country only to those high-school students who grade A, in the top quarter, in the Laboratory's English vocabulary tests. Pursued consistently over a period of years this should in time raise the vocabulary levels of the old established colleges to the point where they challenge the very-high-vocabulary student. Even today the policy gives the high-vocabulary boy or girl the best chance of enjoying college, and of graduating.

Complementing this decision, new schools seem more likely to succeed in solving the formidable problem of the low-vocabulary student. The faculties of recently founded schools are apt to be younger men and women, often with more of the pioneering spirit. As a result the Laboratory decided to recommend the most recently founded colleges only to low-vocabulary students, those who grade D in the Laboratory's tests, in the bottom quarter.

The next question was how to handle what seemed to be obvious exceptions, recently founded colleges thought unquestionably high in vocabulary. This brought up two problems: how to make certain they are high vocabulary; and, second, whether exceptions should be made.

Teaching the low-vocabulary student is one of the pressing problems of education. It should be handled by the most capable faculties of the country. Because those recently

founded schools which seem highest in vocabulary are exactly
the ones most capable of solving the low-vocabulary problem,
it was decided to make no exceptions whatsoever, but to arrange colleges by date of foundation and adhere rigidly to the
policy of recommending the newer colleges to low-vocabulary
high-school students, and old colleges to high-vocabulary ones.

These recommendations rest on the English vocabulary score
of the entering student. They do not show the average vocabulary of the college. Unquestionably some colleges excel others
in teaching methods, in faculty standards. Some take in low-
vocabulary high-school graduates and turn them out high-
vocabulary college graduates; others unfortunately take in
high-vocabulary high-school graduates and turn them out no
more than average college graduates.

A few parents still select a college by name in the belief that
a well-known one is advantageous. The Laboratory believes
that, when a man reaches the age of thirty or thirty-five, when
aptitudes begin gradually to go down, what a man previously
got from college is more important than the name of the college
from which he graduated.

Both English vocabulary and accounting aptitude check
with school and college success; but these two traits are independent variables. Some boys are high vocabulary but low
accounting aptitude, others low vocabulary but high accounting aptitude.

In general the low-accounting-aptitude boy belongs in a
small school, where he is more apt to enter into classroom discussion, ask questions directly, and less likely to be judged
solely by written reports. For the high-accounting-aptitude
boy, who ought to advance at a faster paper-and-pencil speed,
the Laboratory recommends a large school and college.

The following table shows the date of foundation and approximate size of co-educational colleges. Wherever a question arose as to exact date of foundation, either because a school
moved from one city to another, or changed its name, or obtained a charter at a different date from its actual start, or for
any other reason, the Laboratory tries to take the earliest date.
Student bodies change from year to year, but the importance
of this list depends upon the Laboratory recommending each

college to the same type of student persistently from year to year, until student bodies are more uniform than at present. Technical institutes which admit women are listed on pages 138 to 141 of STRUCTURAL VISUALIZATION, and are not repeated here.

The first group of colleges are those founded prior to 1852 and with student bodies in excess of 7100. The Laboratory recommends these to high-vocabulary, high-accounting-aptitude high-school students. The second group of colleges are of approximately the same size but more recent, founded between 1853 and 1871. The Laboratory recommends these to average-vocabulary, high-accounting-aptitude high-school students. The third group, pages 178 to 179, still of the same size but founded since 1872, the Laboratory recommends to low-vocabulary, high-accounting-aptitude students. The fourth group of colleges are once more old, founded prior to 1852, but smaller in size, from 7000 to 3100. The next two groups are of the same size but again more recently founded. The final three groups, pages 181 to 193, are smaller still.

TABLE LXIII

COEDUCATIONAL COLLEGES AND UNIVERSITIES

COLLEGE AND LOCATION DATE FOUNDED	APPROXIMATE STUDENT BODY		
	MEN	WOMEN	TOTAL
Suggested to: Accounting Aptitude, High; English Vocabulary, High			
UNIVERSITY OF PENNSYLVANIA 1740 Philadelphia, Pennsylvania	8,700	2,600	11,300
COLUMBIA UNIVERSITY 1754 New York, New York	11,500	5,500	17,000
UNIVERSITY OF PITTSBURGH 1787 Pittsburgh, Pennsylvania	8,300	4,100	12,400
UNIVERSITY OF MICHIGAN 1817 Ann Arbor, Michigan	8,800	3,800	12,600
UNIVERSITY OF CINCINNATI 1819 Cincinnati, Ohio	7,400	4,100	11,500
INDIANA UNIVERSITY 1820 Bloomington, Indiana	4,400	2,700	7,100
NEW YORK UNIVERSITY 1831 New York, New York	24,200	12,000	36,200

COLLEGE AND LOCATION DATE FOUNDED	APPROXIMATE STUDENT BODY		
	MEN	WOMEN	TOTAL

Continued: Accounting Aptitude, High; English Vocabulary, High

	MEN	WOMEN	TOTAL
BOSTON UNIVERSITY 1839 Boston, Massachusetts	5,900	4,100	10,000
STATE UNIVERSITY OF IOWA 1847 Iowa City, Iowa	4,900	2,500	7,400
COLLEGE OF THE CITY OF NEW YORK 1847 New York, New York	21,400	4,600	26,000
UNIVERSITY OF WISCONSIN 1848 Madison, Wisconsin	8,300	3,700	12,000
NORTHWESTERN UNIVERSITY 1851 Evanston, Illinois	10,000	6,000	16,000

Suggested to: Accounting Aptitude, High; English Vocabulary, Average

	MEN	WOMEN	TOTAL
WASHINGTON UNIVERSITY 1853 St. Louis, Missouri	4,000	3,100	7,100
PENNSYLVANIA STATE COLLEGE 1855 State College, Pennsylvania	5,600	1,500	7,100
LOUISIANA STATE UNIVERSITY 1860 (1845) Baton Rouge, Louisiana	5,700	2,500	8,200
UNIVERSITY OF WASHINGTON 1861 Seattle, Washington	7,600	4,500	12,100
UNIVERSITY OF ILLINOIS 1867 Urbana, Illinois	11,300	3,800	15,100
UNIVERSITY OF CALIFORNIA 1868 (1855) Berkeley and Los Angeles, California	14,000	11,300	25,300
UNIVERSITY OF MINNESOTA 1868 (1851) Minneapolis, Minnesota	11,200	6,200	17,400
UNIVERSITY OF NEBRASKA 1869 Lincoln, Nebraska	4,800	2,600	7,400
SYRACUSE UNIVERSITY 1870 (1849) Syracuse, New York	5,100	3,300	8,400

Suggested to: Accounting Aptitude, High; English Vocabulary, Low

	MEN	WOMEN	TOTAL
OHIO STATE UNIVERSITY 1872 (1870) Columbus, Ohio	10,800	5,100	15,900
UNIVERSITY OF SOUTHERN CALIFORNIA 1880 Los Angeles, California	4,800	2,500	7,300

COLLEGE AND LOCATION DATE FOUNDED	APPROXIMATE STUDENT BODY		
	MEN	WOMEN	TOTAL

Continued: Accounting Aptitude, High; English Vocabulary, Low

	MEN	WOMEN	TOTAL
UNIVERSITY OF TEXAS 1883 (1881) Austin, Texas	7,950	3,550	11,500
TEMPLE UNIVERSITY 1884 Philadelphia, Pennsylvania	7,250	4,650	11,900
UNIVERSITY OF CHICAGO 1890 Chicago, Illinois	6,100	4,500	10,600
WAYNE UNIVERSITY 1929 Detroit, Michigan	7,000	6,000	13,000

Suggested to: Accounting Aptitude, Average; English Vocabulary, High

	MEN	WOMEN	TOTAL
RUTGERS UNIVERSITY 1766 New Brunswick, New Jersey	3,000	1,400	4,400
UNIVERSITY OF GEORGIA 1785 Athens, Georgia	2,200	1,300	3,500
UNIVERSITY OF NORTH CAROLINA 1789 Chapel Hill, North Carolina	3,300	500	3,800
UNIVERSITY OF TENNESSEE 1794 Knoxville, Tennessee	3,300	1,600	4,900
OHIO UNIVERSITY 1804 Athens, Ohio	2,000	1,500	3,500
UNIVERSITY OF MARYLAND 1807 College Park, Maryland	3,300	1,200	4,500
SAINT LOUIS UNIVERSITY 1818 St. Louis, Missouri	3,100	2,400	5,500
GEORGE WASHINGTON UNIVERSITY 1821 Washington, D. C.	4,500	2,300	6,800
MIAMI UNIVERSITY 1824 Oxford, Ohio	1,850	1,300	3,150
WESTERN RESERVE UNIVERSITY 1826 Cleveland, Ohio	2,400	2,300	4,700
UNIVERSITY OF ALABAMA 1831 (1820) Tuscaloosa, Alabama	3,900	1,300	5,200
TULANE UNIVERSITY OF LOUISIANA 1834 New Orleans, Louisiana	3,000	1,600	4,600
UNIVERSITY OF LOUISVILLE 1837 Louisville, Kentucky	2,500	1,500	4,000

COLLEGE AND LOCATION DATE FOUNDED	APPROXIMATE STUDENT BODY		
	MEN	WOMEN	TOTAL

Continued: Accounting Aptitude, Average; English Vocabulary, High

DUKE UNIVERSITY 1838 Durham, North Carolina	2,500	1,100	3,600
UNIVERSITY OF MISSOURI 1839 Columbia, Missouri	4,800	1,400	6,200
BAYLOR UNIVERSITY 1845 Waco, Texas	1,800	1,300	3,100
UNIVERSITY OF BUFFALO 1846 Buffalo, New York	2,850	1,950	4,800
UNIVERSITY OF ROCHESTER 1850 Rochester, New York	1,700	1,500	3,200
UNIVERSITY OF UTAH 1850 Salt Lake City, Utah	2,900	1,600	4,500

Suggested to: Accounting Aptitude, Average; English Vocabulary, Average

UNIVERSITY OF DENVER 1864 Denver, Colorado	2,000	1,800	3,800
CORNELL UNIVERSITY 1865 Ithaca, New York	5,450	1,550	7,000
UNIVERSITY OF KENTUCKY 1865 Lexington, Kentucky	2,700	1,400	4,100
UNIVERSITY OF KANSAS 1866 Lawrence, Kansas	3,200	1,500	4,700
WEST VIRGINIA UNIVERSITY 1867 Morgantown, West Virginia	2,300	900	3,200
LOYOLA UNIVERSITY 1869 Chicago, Illinois	2,400	2,000	4,400
PURDUE UNIVERSITY 1869 Lafayette, Indiana	5,700	1,300	7,000

Suggested to: Accounting Aptitude, Average; English Vocabulary, Low

UNIVERSITY OF OREGON 1872 Eugene, Oregon	2,250	1,350	3,600
UNIVERSITY OF COLORADO 1876 (1861) Boulder, Colorado	3,100	1,400	4,500
UNIVERSITY OF DETROIT 1877 Detroit, Michigan	2,500	800	3,300

COLLEGE AND LOCATION DATE FOUNDED	APPROXIMATE STUDENT BODY		
	MEN	WOMEN	TOTAL

Continued: Accounting Aptitude, Average; English Vocabulary, Low

	MEN	WOMEN	TOTAL
MARQUETTE UNIVERSITY 1881 (1855) Milwaukee, Wisconsin	3,000	1,200	4,200
STANFORD UNIVERSITY 1885 Stanford University, California	3,200	1,400	4,600
UNIVERSITY OF OKLAHOMA 1890 Norman, Oklahoma	4,900	2,100	7,000
DE PAUL UNIVERSITY 1898 Chicago, Illinois	2,300	3,300	5,600
SOUTHERN METHODIST UNIVERSITY 1911 Dallas, Texas	1,900	1,500	3,400
BROOKLYN COLLEGE 1930 Brooklyn, New York	3,250	3,000	6,250

Suggested to: Accounting Aptitude, Low; English Vocabulary, High

	MEN	WOMEN	TOTAL
COLLEGE OF WILLIAM AND MARY IN VIRGINIA 1693 Williamsburg, Virginia	600	600	1,200
WASHINGTON COLLEGE 1706 Chestertown, Maryland	225	125	350
UNIVERSITY OF DELAWARE 1743 Newark, Delaware	600	350	950
BROWN UNIVERSITY 1764 Providence, Rhode Island	1,450	550	2,000
TRANSYLVANIA COLLEGE 1780 Lexington, Kentucky	325	225	550
DICKINSON COLLEGE 1783 Carlisle, Pennsylvania	400	150	550
GEORGETOWN COLLEGE 1787 Georgetown, Kentucky	175	225	400
COLLEGE OF CHARLESTON 1790 Charleston, South Carolina	175	200	375
UNIVERSITY OF VERMONT 1791 Burlington, Vermont	850	550	1,400
TUSCULUM COLLEGE 1794 Greenville, Tennessee	150	150	300
MARIETTA COLLEGE 1797 Marietta, Ohio	250	150	400

COLLEGE AND LOCATION DATE FOUNDED	APPROXIMATE STUDENT BODY		
	MEN	WOMEN	TOTAL
Continued: Accounting Aptitude, Low; English Vocabulary, High			
MIDDLEBURY COLLEGE 1800 Middlebury, Vermont	425	375	800
UNIVERSITY OF SOUTH CAROLINA 1801 Columbia, South Carolina	1,300	600	1,900
ALLEGHENY COLLEGE 1815 Meadville, Pennsylvania	375	325	700
CENTRE COLLEGE OF KENTUCKY 1819 Danville, Kentucky	225	125	350
MARYVILLE COLLEGE 1819 Maryville, Tennessee	350	450	800
UNIVERSITY OF VIRGINIA 1819 Charlottesville, Virginia	2,775	125	2,900
COLBY COLLEGE 1820 Waterville, Maine	425	275	700
CENTENARY COLLEGE OF LOUISIANA 1825 Shreveport, Louisiana	375	275	650
FURMAN UNIVERSITY 1826 Greenville, South Carolina	500	500	1,000
HANOVER COLLEGE 1827 Hanover, Indiana	225	150	375
ILLINOIS COLLEGE 1829 Jacksonville, Illinois	300	100	400
DENISON UNIVERSITY 1831 Granville, Ohio	450	400	850
GETTYSBURG COLLEGE 1832 Gettysburg, Pennsylvania	500	150	650
UNIVERSITY OF RICHMOND 1832 Richmond, Virginia	1,100	300	1,400
KALAMAZOO COLLEGE 1833 Kalamazoo, Michigan	225	150	375
MERCER UNIVERSITY 1833 Macon, Georgia	400	200	600
OBERLIN COLLEGE 1833 Oberlin, Ohio	900	950	1,850
WAGNER MEMORIAL LUTHERAN COL- LEGE 1833 Staten Island, New York	175	100	275

COLLEGE AND LOCATION DATE FOUNDED	APPROXIMATE STUDENT BODY		
	MEN	WOMEN	TOTAL

Continued: Accounting Aptitude, Low; English Vocabulary, High

COLLEGE AND LOCATION DATE FOUNDED	MEN	WOMEN	TOTAL
FRANKLIN COLLEGE 1834 Franklin, Indiana	200	150	350
ALBION COLLEGE 1835 Albion, Michigan	500	325	825
ALFRED UNIVERSITY 1836 Alfred, New York	450	200	650
DEPAUW UNIVERSITY 1837 Greencastle, Indiana	800	600	1,400
GUILFORD COLLEGE 1837 Guilford College, North Carolina	225	125	350
KNOX COLLEGE 1837 Galesburg, Illinois	350	275	625
MARSHALL COLLEGE 1837 Huntington, West Virginia	900	1,000	1,900
MUSKINGUM COLLEGE 1837 New Concord, Ohio	375	375	750
EMORY AND HENRY COLLEGE 1838 Emory, Virginia	250	100	350
ERSKINE COLLEGE 1839 Due West, South Carolina	200	150	350
LORAS COLLEGE 1839 Dubuque, Iowa	400	50	450
BETHANY COLLEGE 1840 Bethany, West Virginia	225	175	400
CARROLL COLLEGE 1840 Waukesha, Wisconsin	400	200	600
SOUTHWESTERN UNIVERSITY 1840 Georgetown, Texas	250	175	425
HOWARD COLLEGE 1842 Birmingham, Alabama	400	275	675
OHIO WESLEYAN UNIVERSITY 1842 Delaware, Ohio	675	775	1,450
ROANOKE COLLEGE 1842 Salem, Virginia	300	100	400
WILLAMETTE UNIVERSITY 1842 Salem, Oregon	525	325	850

| COLLEGE AND LOCATION | APPROXIMATE STUDENT BODY | | |
DATE FOUNDED	MEN	WOMEN	TOTAL

Continued: Accounting Aptitude, Low; English Vocabulary, High

HILLSDALE COLLEGE OF MICHIGAN 1844 Hillsdale, Michigan	225	250	475
IOWA WESLEYAN COLLEGE 1844 Mount Pleasant, Iowa	150	100	250
UNIVERSITY OF MISSISSIPPI 1844 University, Mississippi	950	350	1,300
WITTENBURG COLLEGE 1845 Springfield, Ohio	500	500	1,000
BALDWIN-WALLACE COLLEGE 1845 Berea, Ohio	325	350	675
BELOIT COLLEGE 1846 Beloit, Wisconsin	325	275	600
BUCKNELL UNIVERSITY 1846 Lewisburg, Pennsylvania	850	450	1,300
CARTHAGE COLLEGE 1846 Carthage, Illinois	175	150	325
GRINNELL COLLEGE 1846 Grinnell, Iowa	375	375	750
MOUNT UNION COLLEGE 1846 Alliance, Ohio	375	300	675
EARLHAM COLLEGE 1847 Richmond, Indiana	225	225	450
LAWRENCE COLLEGE 1847 Appleton, Wisconsin	350	350	700
OTTERBEIN COLLEGE 1847 Westerville, Ohio	225	175	400
GENEVA COLLEGE 1848 Beaver Falls, Pennsylvania	325	175	500
SOUTHWESTERN COLLEGE 1848 Memphis, Tennessee	300	175	475
PACIFIC UNIVERSITY 1849 Forest Grove, Oregon	225	125	350
WILLIAM JEWELL COLLEGE 1849 Liberty, Missouri	325	125	450
BUTLER UNIVERSITY 1850 Indianapolis, Indiana	950	800	1,750

COLLEGE AND LOCATION DATE FOUNDED	APPROXIMATE STUDENT BODY		
	MEN	WOMEN	TOTAL

Continued: Accounting Aptitude, Low; English Vocabulary, High

CAPITAL UNIVERSITY 1850 Columbus, Ohio	425	350	775
UNIVERSITY OF DAYTON 1850 Dayton, Ohio	600	100	700
HEIDELBERG COLLEGE 1850 Tiffin, Ohio	225	175	400
HIRAM COLLEGE 1850 Hiram, Ohio	200	150	350
ILLINOIS WESLEYAN UNIVERSITY 1850 Bloomington, Illinois	450	350	800
CARSON-NEWMAN COLLEGE 1851 Jefferson City, Tennessee	225	275	500
CATAWBA COLLEGE 1851 Salisbury, North Carolina	250	250	500
COE COLLEGE 1851 Cedar Rapids, Iowa	450	350	800
COLLEGE OF THE PACIFIC 1851 Stockton, California	275	275	550
HOPE COLLEGE 1851 Holland, Michigan	325	175	500
RIPON COLLEGE 1851 Ripon, Wisconsin	325	175	500
ANTIOCH COLLEGE 1852 Yellow Springs, Ohio	475	275	750
UNIVERSITY OF DUBUQUE 1852 Dubuque, Iowa	275	175	450
TUFTS COLLEGE 1852 Medford, Massachusetts	1,750	350	2,100
WESTMINSTER COLLEGE 1852 New Wilmington, Pennsylvania	300	375	675

Suggested to: Accounting Aptitude, Low; English Vocabulary, Average

CORNELL COLLEGE 1853 Mount Vernon, Iowa	300	325	625
CULVER-STOCKTON COLLEGE 1853 Canton, Missouri	150	100	250

COLLEGE AND LOCATION DATE FOUNDED	APPROXIMATE STUDENT BODY		
	MEN	WOMEN	TOTAL

Continued: Accounting Aptitude, Low; English Vocabulary, Average

COLLEGE AND LOCATION DATE FOUNDED	MEN	WOMEN	TOTAL
EVANSVILLE COLLEGE 1854 Evansville, Indiana	250	200	450
HAMLINE UNIVERSITY 1854 St. Paul, Minnesota	400	250	650
BEREA COLLEGE 1855 Berea, Kentucky	450	400	850
ALBRIGHT COLLEGE 1856 Reading, Pennsylvania	225	150	375
BIRMINGHAM-SOUTHERN COLLEGE 1856 Birmingham, Alabama	600	450	1,050
MONMOUTH COLLEGE 1856 Monmouth, Illinois	325	225	550
NEWBERRY COLLEGE 1856 Newberry, South Carolina	250	150	400
SAINT LAWRENCE UNIVERSITY 1856 Canton, New York	1,325	375	1,700
CENTRAL COLLEGE 1857 Fayette, Missouri	400	250	650
LAKE FOREST COLLEGE 1857 Lake Forest, Illinois	250	125	375
LINFIELD COLLEGE 1857 McMinnville, Oregon	300	300	600
BAKER UNIVERSITY 1858 Baldwin, Kansas	200	175	375
SUSQUEHANNA UNIVERSITY 1858 Selinsgrove, Pennsylvania	200	125	325
VALPARAISO UNIVERSITY 1859 Valparaiso, Indiana	350	150	500
WHITMAN COLLEGE 1859 Walla Walla, Washington	325	275	600
AUGUSTANA COLLEGE 1860 Sioux Falls, South Dakota	250	350	600
AUGUSTANA COLLEGE AND THEOLOGICAL SEMINARY 1860 Rock Island, Illinois	550	400	950
SIMPSON COLLEGE 1860 Indianola, Iowa	225	275	500

COLLEGE AND LOCATION DATE FOUNDED	APPROXIMATE STUDENT BODY		
	MEN	WOMEN	TOTAL

Continued: Accounting Aptitude, Low; English Vocabulary, Average

	MEN	WOMEN	TOTAL
WHEATON COLLEGE 1860 Wheaton, Illinois	600	550	1,150
LUTHER COLLEGE 1861 Decorah, Iowa	350	125	475
NORTH CENTRAL COLLEGE 1861 Naperville, Illinois	350	250	600
GUSTAVUS ADOLPHUS COLLEGE 1862 St. Peter, Minnesota	350	200	550
BATES COLLEGE 1863 Lewiston, Maine	400	300	700
MASSACHUSETTS STATE COLLEGE 1863 Amherst, Massachusetts	950	400	1,350
WILMINGTON COLLEGE 1863 Wilmington, Ohio	125	175	300
SWARTHMORE COLLEGE 1864 Swarthmore, Pennsylvania	375	350	725
UNIVERSITY OF MAINE 1865 Orono, Maine	1,400	500	1,900
OTTAWA UNIVERSITY 1865 Ottawa, Kansas	150	150	300
WASHBURN MUNICIPAL UNIVERSITY 1865 Topeka, Kansas	500	300	800
CARLETON COLLEGE 1866 Northfield, Minnesota	450	425	875
LEBANON VALLEY COLLEGE 1866 Annville, Pennsylvania	300	250	550
UNIVERSITY OF NEW HAMPSHIRE 1866 Durham, New Hampshire	1,350	650	2,000
COLLEGE OF WOOSTER 1866 Wooster, Ohio	500	500	1,000
WESTERN MARYLAND COLLEGE 1867 Westminster, Maryland	275	325	600
TRINITY UNIVERSITY 1869 Waxahachie, Texas	200	150	350
URSINUS COLLEGE 1869 Collegeville, Pennsylvania	275	275	550

| COLLEGE AND LOCATION | APPROXIMATE STUDENT BODY | | |
DATE FOUNDED	MEN	WOMEN	TOTAL

Continued: Accounting Aptitude, Low; English Vocabulary, Average

	MEN	WOMEN	TOTAL
UNIVERSITY OF AKRON 1870 Akron, Ohio	1,050	650	1,700
ELMHURST COLLEGE 1871 Elmhurst, Illinois	225	150	375
OHIO NORTHERN UNIVERSITY 1871 Ada, Ohio	600	200	800

Suggested to: Accounting Aptitude, Low; English Vocabulary, Low

	MEN	WOMEN	TOTAL
UNIVERSITY OF ARKANSAS 1872 Fayetteville, Arkansas	2,050	750	2,800
DOANE COLLEGE 1872 Crete, Nebraska	125	125	250
UNIVERSITY OF THE CITY OF TOLEDO 1872 Toledo, Ohio	1,400	800	2,200
VANDERBILT UNIVERSITY 1872 Nashville, Tennessee	1,350	450	1,800
DRURY COLLEGE 1873 Springfield, Missouri	225	175	400
TEXAS CHRISTIAN UNIVERSITY 1873 Fort Worth, Texas	650	550	1,200
COLORADO COLLEGE 1874 Colorado Springs, Colorado	450	350	800
EMMANUEL MISSIONARY COLLEGE 1874 Berrien Springs, Michigan	200	200	400 .
UNIVERSITY OF NEVADA 1874 Reno, Nevada	750	500	1,250
SAINT OLAF COLLEGE 1874 Northfield, Minnesota	600	500	1,100
BRIGHAM YOUNG UNIVERSITY 1875 Provo, Utah	1,550	1,200	2,750
PARK COLLEGE 1875 Parkville, Missouri	250	250	500
PARSONS COLLEGE 1875 Fairfield, Iowa	175	125	300
CALVIN COLLEGE 1876 Grand Rapids, Michigan	250	200	450

COLLEGE AND LOCATION DATE FOUNDED	APPROXIMATE STUDENT BODY		
	MEN	WOMEN	TOTAL

Continued: Accounting Aptitude, Low; English Vocabulary, Low

COLLEGE AND LOCATION	MEN	WOMEN	TOTAL
GROVE CITY COLLEGE 1876 Grove City, Pennsylvania	525	400	925
HENDRIX COLLEGE 1876 Conway, Arkansas	225	175	400
JUNIATA COLLEGE 1876 Huntingdon, Pennsylvania	275	175	450
ASHLAND COLLEGE 1878 Ashland, Ohio	175	175	350
CREIGHTON UNIVERSITY 1878 Omaha, Nebraska	1,100	300	1,400
DUQUESNE UNIVERSITY 1878 Pittsburgh, Pennsylvania	1,900	1,100	3,000
UNION COLLEGE 1879 Barbourville, Kentucky	250	200	450
BRIDGEWATER COLLEGE 1880 Bridgewater, Virginia	150	125	275
CENTRAL Y.M.C.A. COLLEGE 1880 Chicago, Illinois	2,450	550	3,000
SOUTHERN UNIV. & AGRICULTURAL AND MECH. COLL. 1880 Scotlandville, La.	350	425	775
BETHANY COLLEGE 1881 Lindsborg, Kansas	150	175	325
UNIVERSITY OF CONNECTICUT 1881 Storrs, Connecticut	850	400	1,250
DRAKE UNIVERSITY 1881 Des Moines, Iowa	850	550	1,400
FENN COLLEGE 1881 Cleveland, Ohio	2,700	100	2,800
YANKTON COLLEGE 1881 Yankton, South Dakota	200	150	350
COLLEGE OF EMPORIA 1882 Emporia, Kansas	175	175	350
FINDLAY COLLEGE 1882 Findlay, Ohio	175	100	275
HASTINGS COLLEGE 1882 Hastings, Nebraska	300	350	650

COLLEGE AND LOCATION DATE FOUNDED	APPROXIMATE STUDENT BODY		
	MEN	WOMEN	TOTAL

Continued: Accounting Aptitude, Low; English Vocabulary, Low

COLLEGE AND LOCATION DATE FOUNDED	MEN	WOMEN	TOTAL
PACIFIC UNION COLLEGE 1882 Angwin, California	300	275	575
UNIVERSITY OF SOUTH DAKOTA 1882 Vermillion, South Dakota	550	350	900
DAKOTA WESLEYAN UNIVERSITY 1883 Mitchell, South Dakota	250	200	450
HOUGHTON COLLEGE 1883 Houghton, New York	225	200	425
HURON COLLEGE 1883 Huron, South Dakota	175	100	275
JAMESTOWN COLLEGE 1883 Jamestown, North Dakota	200	200	400
UNIVERSITY OF NORTH DAKOTA 1883 Grand Forks, North Dakota	1,400	600	2,000
SIOUX FALLS COLLEGE 1883 Sioux Falls, South Dakota	200	150	350
JOHN B. STETSON UNIVERSITY 1883 DeLand, Florida	400	450	850
TARKIO COLLEGE 1883 Tarkio, Missouri	150	100	250
AMERICAN INTERNATIONAL COLLEGE 1885 Springfield, Massachusetts	350	300	650
UNIVERSITY OF ARIZONA 1885 Tucson, Arizona	1,850	1,050	2,900
MACALESTER COLLEGE 1885 St. Paul, Minnesota	375	325	700
ROLLINS COLLEGE 1885 Winter Park, Florida	200	225	425
SOUTHWESTERN COLLEGE 1885 Winfield, Kansas	275	300	575
ALMA COLLEGE 1886 Alma, Michigan	250	150	400
UNIVERSITY OF CHATTANOOGA 1886 Chattanooga, Tennessee	400	425	825
FLORIDA SOUTHERN COLLEGE 1886 Lakeland, Florida	200	650	850

COLLEGE AND LOCATION DATE FOUNDED	APPROXIMATE STUDENT BODY		
	MEN	WOMEN	TOTAL

Continued: Accounting Aptitude, Low; English Vocabulary, Low

COLLEGE AND LOCATION DATE FOUNDED	MEN	WOMEN	TOTAL
BETHEL COLLEGE 1887 North Newton, Kansas	200	175	375
CATHOLIC UNIVERSITY OF AMERICA 1887 Washington, D. C.	1,550	550	2,100
NEBRASKA WESLEYAN UNIVERSITY 1887 Lincoln, Nebraska	225	225	450
OCCIDENTAL COLLEGE 1887 Los Angeles, California	400	400	800
POMONA COLLEGE 1887 Claremont, California	425	400	825
UNIVERSITY OF WYOMING 1887 Laramie, Wyoming	1,400	800	2,200
COLLEGE OF PUGET SOUND 1888 Tacoma, Washington	400	300	700
UNIVERSITY OF IDAHO 1889 Moscow, Idaho	2,200	800	3,000
MANCHESTER COLLEGE 1889 North Manchester, Indiana	325	350	675
MISSOURI VALLEY COLLEGE 1889 Marshall, Missouri	150	125	275
MORNINGSIDE COLLEGE 1889 Sioux City, Iowa	325	250	575
GEORGE WILLIAMS COLLEGE 1890 Chicago, Illinois	200	75	275
WHITWORTH COLLEGE 1890 Spokane, Washington	125	100	225
COLLEGE OF IDAHO 1891 Caldwell, Idaho	250	150	400
CONCORDIA COLLEGE 1891 Moorhead, Minnesota	275	250	525
HARDIN-SIMMONS UNIVERSITY 1891 Abilene, Texas	425	375	800
LENOIR RHYNE COLLEGE 1891 Hickory, North Carolina	250	250	500
SEATTLE PACIFIC COLLEGE 1891 Seattle, Washington	150	225	375

COLLEGE AND LOCATION DATE FOUNDED	APPROXIMATE STUDENT BODY		
	MEN	WOMEN	TOTAL

Continued: Accounting Aptitude, Low; English Vocabulary, Low

UNION COLLEGE 1891 Lincoln, Nebraska	200	250	450
MILLSAPS COLLEGE 1892 Jackson, Mississippi	400	200	600
UNIVERSITY OF NEW MEXICO 1892 Albuquerque, New Mexico	1,100	700	1,800
WALLA WALLA COLLEGE 1892 College Place, Washington	325	275	600
AMERICAN UNIVERSITY 1893 Washington, D. C.	1,450	950	2,400
AURORA COLLEGE 1893 Aurora, Illinois	100	100	200
UPSALA COLLEGE 1893 East Orange, New Jersey	225	175	400
UNIVERSITY OF TULSA 1894 Tulsa, Oklahoma	700	400	1,100
MONTANA STATE UNIVERSITY 1895 Missoula, Montana	1,400	800	2,200
MUNICIPAL UNIVERSITY OF WICHITA 1895 Wichita, Kansas	975	625	1,600
SO. CAROLINA STATE AGRICULTURAL & MECH. COLL. 1896 Orangeburg, S. C.	400	400	800
LINCOLN MEMORIAL UNIVERSITY 1897 Harrogate, Tennessee	250	200	450
SEATTLE COLLEGE 1898 Seattle, Washington	350	300	650
SOUTHWESTERN LOUISIANA INSTITUTE 1898 Lafayette, Louisiana	1,200	800	2,000
FORT HAYS KANSAS STATE COLLEGE 1901 Hays, Kansas	625	475	1,100
WHITTIER COLLEGE 1901 Whittier, California	300	300	600
JAMES MILLIKIN UNIVERSITY 1901 Decatur, Illinois	350	300	650
LYNCHBURG COLLEGE 1903 Lynchburg, Virginia	200	100	300

COLLEGE AND LOCATION DATE FOUNDED	APPROXIMATE STUDENT BODY		
	MEN	WOMEN	TOTAL

Continued: Accounting Aptitude, Low; English Vocabulary, Low

COLLEGE AND LOCATION DATE FOUNDED	MEN	WOMEN	TOTAL
LOUISIANA COLLEGE 1906 Pineville, Louisiana	250	150	400
UNIVERSITY OF HAWAII 1907 Honolulu, Hawaii	1,200	1,300	2,500
PHILLIPS UNIVERSITY 1907 Enid, Oklahoma	400	450	850
BILLINGS POLYTECHNIC INSTITUTE 1908 Billings, Montana	350	400	750
UNIVERSITY OF REDLANDS 1909 Redlands, California	375	350	725
ARKANSAS STATE COLLEGE 1910 Jonesboro, Arkansas	800	600	1,400
BOWLING GREEN STATE UNIVERSITY 1910 Bowling Green, Ohio	650	650	1,300
WESTERN STATE COLLEGE OF COLORADO 1911 Gunnison, Colorado	250	200	450
REED COLLEGE 1911 Portland, Oregon	300	250	550
KENT STATE UNIVERSITY 1912 Kent, Ohio	1,300	1,300	2,600
RICE INSTITUTE 1912 (1891) Houston, Texas	1,000	400	1,400
NORTHWEST NAZARENE COLLEGE 1913 Nampa, Idaho	200	200	400
HUMBOLDT STATE COLLEGE 1914 Arcata, California	200	200	400
UNIVERSITY OF ALASKA 1915 College, Alaska	200	100	300
CHAPMAN COLLEGE 1920 Los Angeles, California	175	175	350
UNIVERSITY OF KANSAS CITY 1933 Kansas City, Missouri	600	400	1,000
BLACK MOUNTAIN COLLEGE 1933 Black Mountain, North Carolina	15	50	65
GEORGE PEPPERDINE COLLEGE 1937 Los Angeles, California	175	100	275

INDEX

PUBLICATIONS

Square Pegs in Square Holes *by Margaret E. Broadley;*
Doubleday, 1946. *Two dollars and fifty cents.*

Concerning the grammar-school pupil, as well as the adult.
Aptitudes and the Languages *by Johnson O'Connor;*
Human Engineering Laboratory, 1944. *Two dollars.*

Concerning the high-school and college student, as well as the adult.
Structural Visualization *by Johnson O'Connor;*
Human Engineering Laboratory, 1942. *Four dollars.*

The Too-Many-Aptitude Woman *by Johnson O'Connor;*
Human Engineering Laboratory, 1941. *Four dollars.*

The Unique Individual *by Johnson O'Connor;*
Human Engineering Laboratory, 1947. *Four dollars.*

Concerning primarily the problems of the adult.
Unsolved Business Problems *by Johnson O'Connor;*
Human Engineering Laboratory, 1940. *Four dollars.*
   This book replaces Born That Way.

Ideaphoria *by Johnson O'Connor;*
Human Engineering Laboratory, 1944. *Four dollars.*

For the general reader.
Johnson O'Connor English Vocabulary Builder, Two Volumes;
Human Engineering Laboratory, 1948. *Six dollars per volume.*

The Laboratory's mathematical techniques.
Psychometrics *by Johnson O'Connor;*
Harvard University Press, 1934. *Three dollars and fifty cents.*

Out of print.
Born That Way *by Johnson O'Connor;*
Williams and Wilkins, 1928.

In preparation.
The Scientist *by Johnson O'Connor.* *Four dollars.*

TECHNICAL REPORTS

English Vocabulary

5 First Revision of Form E of the English Vocabulary Test, Worksample 95 (1935)

11 Construction of the English Vocabulary Test, Worksample 95, Form DB *by Mary E. Filley* (1939)

33 English Vocabulary Distributions for Twenty-nine Secondary Schools, Worksample 95, Form EA *by Marie V. Alfano* (1939)

35 Variation of Vocabulary Scores with Age and Schooling, Worksample 95 *by Marie V. Alfano* (1939)

36 Variation of Vocabulary Scores with Age, Sex, and Schooling, Worksample 95 *by Marie V. Alfano* (1939)

41 Revision of Form AB Leading to Forms AC and AD, Worksample 95 *by Mary E. Filley* (1939)

42 Revision of Form F Leading to Forms FA and FB, Worksample 95 *by Mary E. Filley* (1939)

43 Revision of Form BA Leading to Forms BB and BC, Worksample 95 *by Mary E. Filley* (1939)

53 Revision of Form G Leading to Form GA, Worksample 95 *by Mary E. Filley* (1940)

55 Revision of Form EA Leading to Form EB, Worksample 95 *by Mary E. Filley* (1940)

57 Revision of Form A Leading to Form AA, Worksample 180 *by Mary E. Filley* (1940)

58 English Vocabulary Distributions Converted to the General Scale for Forty-two Secondary Schools *by Edward H. Sidserf* (1940)

59 Revision of Form AA Leading to Form AB, Worksample 180 *by Mary E. Filley* (1941)

62 Revision of Form A Leading to Form AA, Worksample 271 *by Mary E. Filley* (1940)

63 Revision of Form CB Leading to Form CC, Worksample 95 *by Mary E. Filley* (1940)

64 Revision of Form B Leading to Form BA, Worksample 176 *by Mary E. Filley* (1940)

66 Revision of Form AA Leading to Form AB, Worksample 176 *by Mary E. Filley* (1940)

67 Revision of Forms B and BA Leading to Form BB, Worksample 180 *by Mary E. Filley* (1940)

72 Index to Test Words of Vocabulary Worksamples *by Edward H. Sidserf* (1940)

73 Test Words and Misleads Classifications of Vocabulary Forms G, H, and I, Worksample 95 *by Mary E. Filley* (1940)

76 Revision of Form B Leading to Form BA, Worksample 271 *by Mary E. Filley* (1941)

80 The Construction of the English Vocabulary Test, Worksample 311, Form A *by Mary E. Filley* (1941)

84 Report I—The 95 EA Scale and the General Scale for the English Vocabulary Tests.

Report II—Relation between Recognition and Active Vocabularies *by Edward H. Sidserf* (1941)

94 Learning Process in English Vocabulary as shown by Words of Similar Sound *by F. L. McLanathan* (1941)—Volume I

Experimental Tests

Judgment

6 Revision of Form A of Worksample 169, Judgment in Social Situations (1936)
15 Statistical and Graphical Analysis of Three Forms of Worksample 169, Judgment in Social Situations (1938)
108 Progress Report on Judgment, Worksamples 276, 277, 278, and Deductive Reasoning, Worksample 248 *by John M. Howe* (1942)

Left Sidedness

114 A Study of the Hand and Eye Dominance Test *by Dorothy and Ellen Pano* (1942)
232 A Study of Left-Sidedness *by Marie H. Licht* (1946)
246 The Effect of Cross Dominance on Accounting Aptitude *by Priscilla Schaff* (1946)

Memory

21 Steps Toward the Isolation of Tonal Memory as a Mental Element (1938)
22 The Measurement of Number Memory (1938)
37 Two Experiments in the Measure of Memory for Design *by Samuel P. Horton* (1939)
60 Experiments and Research on the Production of Tonal Memory Records *by P. J. Quinn* (1940)
70 Research Progress on the Number Memory Test, with a Research Program Applicable to Any Test, Worksample 165 *by Samuel P. Horton* (1940)
91 The Visual Number Span Test, Worksample 239, Form B *by John M. Howe* (1941)
105 Internal Analysis of the Memory for Design Test, Worksample 294 II *by William H. Helme* (1942)
178 The Relationship Between Tonal Memory and Pitch Discrimination *by Marie H. Licht* (1945)
197 A Report in the Procurement of Norms for Worksample 366 Form AB, Rhythm Memory (1947)
238 A Study of Tonal Memory and Pitch Discrimination *by Marie H. Licht* (1946)
279 The Relation of Time to Correct Lines in Worksample 294 Form U, Memory for Design *by Dorothy Belmont* (1946)
372 Revision of Memory for Design Worksample 294 Form UA Leading to Form UB *by Ruth Reshall* (1947)

Observation

10 The Observation Test, Worksample 184 (1936)
51 First Experiments in Developing a Second Measure of Observation, Worksample 206 *by Samuel P. Horton* (1940)
52 Experimental Reduction of the Influence of Observation in the Black Cube Assembly with Worksample 210 *by Samuel P. Horton* (1940)
106 Analysis of the Observation Test, Worksample 206 *by William H. Helme* (1942)
136 Percentiles for Observation Worksample 206 for Males and Females *by Dorothy Pano* (1944)

Number

46   Relationships Among Nineteen Group Tests and Their Validity for Freshmen Engineering Marks *by Samuel P. Horton* (1939)

75   Conversion of College Entrance Rating Scale Words into Their Genus and Species of the Residues of Vilfredo Pareto *by H. A. Zantow* (1940)

77   An Analysis of the Scores of Eight Stock-Traders *by Evelyn C. Wight* (1941)

81   Report I—Analysis of the Worksample Scores of Forty-nine Accountants; Report II—Follow-up of Twenty-five Accountants; Report III—Composite Scoring Scale for Number Checking and Wiggly Block, Worksamples 1 and 5 *by Leonard C. Seeley* (1941)

90   An Analysis of the Worksample Scores of 101 High-School Teachers *by Leonard C. Seeley* (1941)

96   Analysis of the Worksample Scores of Seventy-six Educational Advisers in the Civilian Conservation Corps *by Leonard C. Seeley* (1941)

97   A Follow-up of the Careers of Tested Engineering Students—Volume I—(A Preliminary Survey of the Test Scores of Groups Classified by Their Records in the Educational Phase of Their Careers) *by Samuel P. Horton* (1941); Volume II—(Occupational Success of 203 Men in Relation to Their Test Scores Obtained When They Were Students) *by Samuel P. Horton* (1942); Volume III—(A Continuation of the Study of the Occupational Careers of 203 Men to Test Scores Obtained from Them as Students) *by Samuel P. Horton* (1943)

100   Preliminary Report on a Statistical Study of the Stevens Defense Industries School Group—First Session *by Samuel P. Horton* (1942)

101   Analysis of the Worksample Scores of 109 Engineers *by Leonard C. Seeley* (1942)

102   Preliminary Study of the Relationship of Test Scores to Success or Failure in School *by Mary O. Luqueer* (1942)

107   Report to the U. S. War Department on Tests for Trainability in the War Industries Training School *by Samuel P. Horton* (1942)

113   A Study of the Correlations between Worksamples 1, 4 and 5, 16, 18, and 35 Form AE, with High-School Subjects *by Katherine J. Rippere* (1943)

119   Analysis of the Worksample Scores of Sixty-two Stenographers *by Eva Muller* (1944)

128   An Investigation in Follow-up *by Anson DuBois* (1945)

237   Occupations *by Alice Stone* (1946)

Each Technical Report, two dollars.

VOCABULARY TEST FORMS

Applicable fifth grade to second year high school.
Junior English Vocabulary, Worksample 176, Form AC
Junior English Vocabulary, Worksample 176, Form BA

Applicable first year high school through college.
English Vocabulary, Worksample 95, Form AD
English Vocabulary, Worksample 95, Form BC
English Vocabulary, Worksample 95, Form CC
English Vocabulary, Worksample 95, Form DB
English Vocabulary, Worksample 95, Form EB
English Vocabulary, Worksample 95, Form GB

Five dollars per hundred. Single copies not sold.
Each initial order must include an additional two dollars to cover Administration of Vocabulary Tests *which gives norms and interpretation.*

All of these may be obtained through the
Human Engineering Laboratory Incorporated
347 Beacon Street Boston 16 Massachusetts.

CPSIA information can be obtained at www.ICGtesting.com
Printed in the USA
LVOW010556210313

325326LV00004B/681/P